MW01658100

Soups and Stews

The Confident Cooking Promise of Success

Welcome to the world of Confident Cooking, where recipes are double-tested by our team of home economists to achieve a high standard of success—and delicious results every time.

bay books

C O N T E

Pea and Ham Soup, page 12

Clam Chowder, page 36

Cioppino, page 98

Roasted Pumpkin Soup, page 37

N T S

Creamy Chicken with Mushrooms, page 108

Creamy Beetroot Soup, page 30

The Publisher thanks the following for their assistance in the photography for this book: Home and Garden on the Mall; Pacific East India Company; B.J. Homewares; Waterford Wedgwood; Villeroy & Boch; Primex, Marinvale; Milners; House at Newtown; Made in Japan; Accoutrement.

Chilli con Carne, page 94

Rich Steak and Kidney Stew, page 110

All recipes in this book have been double-tested.

When we test our recipes, we rate them for ease of preparation. The following cookery ratings are on the recipes in this book, making them easy to use and understand.

A single Cooking with Confidence symbol indicates a recipe that is simple and generally quick to make – perfect for beginners.

Two symbols indicate the need for just a little more care and a little more time.

Three symbols indicate special dishes that need more investment in time, care and patience—but the results are worth it.

IMPORTANT

Those who might be at risk from the effects of salmonella food poisoning (the elderly, pregnant women, young children and those suffering from immume deficiency diseases) should consult their doctor with any concerns about eating raw eggs.

Soup & Stew Secrets

There are no secret tricks to making wonderful soups and stews... no fancy techniques or difficult finishes... just a kitchen filled with delicious aromas and a tender, flavoursome meal that will satisfy the whole family from one pot.

Soups and stews are versatile, varied and above all delicious. Fish and fowl, meat and pulses, vegetables and even fruit can all be prepared in these ways. Once you have mastered the basics you will quickly realise that most soups or stews, from the humblest to the most exotic, are put together along similar lines. The differences lie in the ingredients and embellishments. We are all envious of those confident casual cooks who can just throw a few ingredients into the pot and produce a richly fragrant sauce packed with tender meat and flavoursome vegetables. But once you have gained confidence with the techniques you will find it easy to adapt them for your own variations. For example, many soups are blended in a food processor, (always let the soup cool a little first, so that you won't splash yourself with scalding liquid), but you may like to vary the textures by leaving some of the soup unpuréed.

Always pick the best ingredients. Your soup or stew is only as good as the sum of its parts. Use fresh bright-coloured meat and pick fresh firm vegetables that are in season

COATING AND BROWNING MEAT

By coating the meat in seasoned flour and then browning it on all sides in oil or butter you will give it a crisp brown coating and delicious taste. The flour also helps to thicken the liquid—usually once you have coated the meat in flour you won't need to use another thickener. (If you find at the end of cooking you still need to thicken the soup or stew a little more it is always better to reduce the liquid by fast simmering for a while, uncovered, rather than adding more flour.)

Don't coat the meat until you are ready to start cooking or the moisture in the meat will absorb the flour. It will no longer be a coating and could change the whole texture of the dish. If the flour *is* absorbed for some reason, re-coat the meat just before use and shake off any excess.

To coat meat in flour you can lay the flour on greaseproof paper, sprinkle with a little seasoning and then turn the meat in the flour with your fingers or a pair of tongs. A cleverer and less messy method is to put the seasoned flour in a bag, add the meat cubes in batches, shake and then pick out the meat. Shake off any excess flour.

Browning the meat also seals in the juices and gives a good rich colour to the stew. Meat is browned quickly over fairly high heat and turned often to prevent sticking and to brown all sides. Oil is often used rather than butter, as butter burns at a lower temperature. However, a combination of the two means the oil prevents the butter burning and the butter adds flavour to the coating. It may be necessary to brown the meat in batches if there is a lot of it—too much meat crowded into the pan will merely stew in its own juices and become tough.

An easy way to coat meat with flour is to put them both in a bag and shake.

Brown meat quickly on all sides, over high heat, to seal in the juices.

CHEAP EATS

You may be using the freshest ingredients you can find but they certainly don't need to be the most expensive. One of the great advantages of soups and stews is that they are generally better made with the more economical cuts of meat. Unlike expensive cuts, which are usually cooked quickly, the cheaper cuts of meat are best when slowly simmered in liquid as the process tenderises the meat. You can tell when the meat is cooked because the pieces will break up easily with a fork. Beef cuts such as blade, chuck, round or topside steak are ideal and generally have more flavour than fillet or rump. Some of the lamb cuts which we rarely use are ideal for producing tasty stews—neck chops and lamb shanks are perfect and easy on the budget. Trim away any excess fat and sinew—these will toughen during cooking and can cause the meat to shrink. Cut the meat into even-sized pieces that will cook at the same rate. About 2–3 cm (3/4–1 1/4 inch) cubes is probably best, any smaller and the meat will fall into shreds while cooking and not look as appetising. Any chicken pieces are suitable for stews, but take care they are simmered gently, not boiled, or the meat will toughen.

SIMMERING

Generally, when making soups or stews the ingredients are browned, liquid is added and the food is brought to the boil. The heat is then reduced and the pan covered and left to simmer slowly until the ingredients are tender. Fish soups and stews are different in that the sauce is often prepared first and the fish added later to ensure it is not overcooked, tough or dry. Fast-cooking vegetables, such as snow peas, broccoli or mushrooms, are also usually added towards the end of cooking to prevent them becoming too soft.

Soups and stews should never be boiled for long periods, or the meat will become tough and stringy and lose its flavour and any vegetables will break up. A lazy simmer is best—tiny bubbles will appear at a slower pace on the surface of the food.

By the time a stew is cooked there is quite likely to be a thin layer of fat on the surface which you can easily skim off with a spoon or some paper towels to make the dish healthier. This is even easier if you are refrigerating the dish overnight—the fat will set and can be lifted off.

A dish is boiling when large bubbles appear in quick succession.

Soups and stews are best cooked at a lazy simmer.

PANS

When choosing a pan for making soups and stews, buy one that can be taken straight from the freezer to the stove or oven. A pan with a heavy base ensures an even distribution of heat which is important when dishes are simmering in liquid for a long time. A tight-fitting lid is essential to keep in moisture. The size of the dish is important. If it's too small the liquid might overflow, too large and the food will dry out because the liquid will reduce too quickly. The food should come approximately three-quarters of the way up the dish for the best result.

SEASONING

When making both soups and stews it is best to add seasoning at the end of the cooking process. Often the liquid has been reduced during simmering which makes the flavours more concentrated. Chilled soups should be tasted after chilling and may need more seasoning than hot soups. Some dishes thicken if left to stand and may need to have water added to bring them back to the right consistency—don't forget to taste for seasoning.

Don't sprinkle salt directly onto raw meat before cooking as it draws out the moisture and can make the meat tough and dry.

STORING AND FREEZING

For busy cooks, a great advantage of soups and stews is that both methods lend themselves to cooking in batches and storing. Fish soups and stews and the delicate oriental soups should be eaten immediately: their textures and flavours disintegrate on reheating. But most meat dishes, especially those which are highly spiced, such as curries, positively benefit from being refrigerated for a day or two before serving. This lets the flavours mature and also gives you the opportunity to easily lift off any fat which may have formed on the surface of the dish.

Many stews and some soups can be successfully frozen for 1 to 3 months. Don't add cream before freezing as it can curdle. Add it when you reheat to serve.

The food should be frozen as soon as it has cooled—and it should be cooled as quickly as possible to prevent bacteria forming. Skim any fat from the surface before freezing. The easiest way to freeze a soup or stew is to put a plastic bag inside a jug or bowl, spoon the food into it, tie loosely and then put the jug or bowl in the freezer. When the food has frozen, remove the bag from the container, squeeze out as much air as possible and seal securely. Label and date it before returning it to the freezer. If you are cooking in bulk it may be sensible to divide it into portions that can be thawed singly.

It is always best to thaw food completely before reheating but if you are in a hurry it is possible to reheat straight from the freezer. Remove from the bag or container and heat slowly in a pan or microwave for about 20 minutes depending on the amount.

Line a jug or bowl with a plastic bag and spoon in the soup or stew.

Seal the bag and label with the date, then freeze and remove the jug.

Stock

The secret to great soup is good stock. Home-made stock will give your soups a richer, more flavoursome base and, although the cooking time is long, the preparation couldn't be easier. Browning meat bones beforehand adds flavour and colour and a fresh bouquet garni of parsley, thyme and a bay leaf tied in muslin is preferable to the dried, bought variety. Make double the amount of stock and keep some frozen in an ice tray to be on hand whenever you need it. Stock should never be boiled: this will impair the flavour. Allow it to simmer gently.

CHICKEN STOCK

Preparation time: 20 minutes
Total cooking time: 3 hours 50 minutes
Makes 1.5 litres (6 cups)

1.5 kg (3 lb 5 oz) chicken bones
2 large onions, unpeeled and roughly chopped
3 litres (12 cups) water
2 medium carrots, unpeeled and roughly chopped
2 sticks celery, leaves included, roughly chopped
1 bouquet garni
12 black or white peppercorns

1 Preheat the oven to 180°C (350°F/Gas 4). Bake the chicken bones and the onions in a large baking dish for 50 minutes, or until well browned. Transfer the bones and onion to a large heavy-based pan or stockpot.
2 Add the water, vegetables, bouquet garni and peppercorns to the pan. Bring slowly to the boil, then reduce the heat and simmer, uncovered, for 3 hours, skimming any froth from the top of the stock if necessary. Strain the stock through a fine sieve and discard the bones and vegetables.
3 Pour the stock into a shallow dish so that it cools quickly and then refrigerate until completely cold. Remove any fat that sets on the top.

FISH STOCK

Preparation time: 15 minutes
Total cooking time: 30 minutes
Makes 1.5 litres (6 cups)

15 g (1/2 oz) butter
2 medium onions, finely chopped
2 litres (8 cups) water
1.5 kg (3 lb 5 oz) fish bones, heads and tails
10 black peppercorns
1 bouquet garni

1 Melt the butter in a large heavy-based pan and add the onion. Cook, stirring, over low heat for 10 minutes until the onion is soft and transparent, but not browned.
2 Add the water, fish, peppercorns and bouquet garni and bring slowly to the boil. Reduce the heat and simmer, uncovered, for 20 minutes, frequently skimming any froth from the surface. Strain the stock through a fine sieve, discarding the bones and vegetables, and leave to cool before refrigerating.
Note: Use a white-fleshed fish for stock. Darker-fleshed, oily fish tends to make the stock greasy.

VEGETABLE STOCK

Preparation time: 15 minutes
Total cooking time: 1 hour 30 minutes
Makes 1.5 litres (6 cups)

2 tablespoons oil
4 large brown onions, unpeeled and chopped
5 large carrots, unpeeled and chopped
2 large parsnips, unpeeled and chopped
5 sticks celery, including leaves, chopped
2 bay leaves
fresh bouquet garni
1 teaspoon whole black peppercorns
3 litres (12 cups) water

1 Preheat the oven to 200°C (400°F/Gas 6). Heat the oil in a large baking dish, add the chopped onion, carrot and parsnip and toss to coat in the oil. Bake for 30 minutes, until lightly golden.

2 Transfer the baked vegetables to a large heavy-based pan. Add the remaining ingredients and bring to the boil slowly. Reduce the heat and simmer, uncovered, for 1 hour, until reduced by half.

3 Strain the stock through a fine sieve, discarding the vegetables. Leave to cool before refrigerating. Remove any fat which sets on the top.

BEEF STOCK

Preparation time: 20 minutes
Total cooking time: 4 hours 50 minutes
Makes 1 litre (4 cups)

2 kg (4 lb 8 oz) beef bones
2 carrots, unpeeled and roughly chopped
2 brown onions, unpeeled and roughly chopped
3 litres (12 cups) water
2 sticks celery, leaves included, roughly chopped
1 bouquet garni
12 black peppercorns

1 Preheat the oven to 200°C (400°F/Gas 6). Place the beef bones in a large baking dish and bake for 30 minutes, turning occasionally. Add the carrot and onion to the dish and cook for another 20 minutes.

2 Transfer the bones, carrot and onion to a stockpot or large heavy-based pan. Drain the excess fat from the baking dish then pour 250 ml (1 cup) of the water into the dish. Stir gently with a wooden spoon to dissolve any pan juices and then add to the stockpot.

3 Add the celery, remaining water, bouquet garni and peppercorns to the stockpot. Bring slowly to the boil and then reduce the heat and leave to simmer, uncovered, for 4 hours. Occasionally skim away any froth that forms on the top of the stock.

4 Strain the stock through a fine sieve and discard the vegetables and bones. Pour into a clean shallow dish so that the stock cools quickly, (you could then leave this dish to stand in a larger oven tray of cold water if the weather is very warm) then put in the refrigerator. Once the stock is cold it is easier to lift off any fat which may set on the top.

RATATOUILLE AND PASTA SOUP WITH GARLIC SIPPETS

BOUILLABAISSE WITH AIOLI

TOMATO SOUP WITH PESTO

Garnishes

If you are preparing soup to serve as a dinner party starter or as a main course meal for the family, liven it up a little by adding bowls of accompaniments in the centre of the table. People can pick and choose what to add to their own bowl of soup. Croutons and Garlic Sippets are a delicious way to add extra texture and interest to just about any soup. Rouille and Aioli are best known as creamy, garlicky toppings for fish soups. Harissa is great for spicing up pumpkin soup and Pesto is perfect on thick vegetable soups. You could try serving toppings with stews as well.

AIOLI

Put 2 egg yolks in a food processor. Add 3 peeled, crushed cloves of garlic and 2 teaspoons lemon juice and process for 20 seconds. With the motor running add 250 ml (1 cup) light olive oil in a thin steady stream and continue processing until the mixture is thick and creamy. Add 2 extra teaspoons of lemon juice and season to taste. Aioli is served in dollops on top of soups and can be stored in an airtight container in the refrigerator for up to 3 weeks.

GARLIC SIPPETS

Trim the crusts from 3 slices of white or brown bread and cut the bread into small cubes. Heat 60 ml (1/4 cup) olive oil in a small, heavy-based pan. Add 1–2 crushed cloves of garlic. When the oil is moderately hot add the bread cubes in batches. Cook until golden and crisp, then remove from the pan with a slotted spoon and leave to drain on paper towels while frying the rest. Sprinkle over soup.

PESTO

Put 2–3 cloves of garlic, 60 g (2 cups) of fresh basil leaves, 50 g (1/2 cup) of freshly grated Parmesan cheese, 2 tablespoons toasted pinenuts and 125 ml (1/2 cup) of olive oil in a food processor. Process to form a paste, adding a little extra oil to thin if necessary. Spoon the pesto sparingly over soup in serving bowls. Store in an airtight, screw-top jar. Pack the pesto firmly into the jar and pour in enough extra olive oil to cover the surface. Refrigerate for up to 2 weeks.

PUMPKIN SOUP WITH HARISSA

SPINACH AND POTATO SOUP WITH CROUTONS

SMOKED FISH CHOWDER WITH ROUILLE

ROUILLE

Remove the crusts from 4 thick slices of white bread. Put the bread in a bowl and just cover with water. Leave to soak for 5 minutes then drain, squeezing out the water. Put the bread in a food processor with 4 cloves of garlic, 2 chopped red chillies, 2 egg yolks, salt and pepper. Process for 20 seconds and then, with the motor still running, add 185 ml (3/4 cup) of olive oil in a thin steady stream. Process until thick and creamy, adding 1 small peeled red capsicum (pepper) if you like. Serve in dollops on top of fish soups.

Hint: To peel a capsicum, cut in half and remove the seeds and membrane. Brush the skin with a little oil and grill (broil), skin side up, under high heat until the skin blackens. Leave to cool under a clean tea towel, then peel away the skin and discard.

HARISSA

Split 100 g (3 1/2 oz) dried red chillies in half and remove the seeds—wear rubber or cotton gloves to do this or later you'll rub your eyes or mouth and find them smarting with hot chilli. Place the chillies in hot water to soften and rehydrate slightly. Drain the chillies and put them in a food processor or blender with 6 cloves of garlic, 4 tablespoons salt, 50 g (1/2 cup) of ground coriander and 35 g (1/3 cup) of ground cumin. Process for 30 seconds. Add 170 ml (2/3 cup) of olive oil in a thin steady stream, processing as you do so until the mixture forms a paste. Store in an airtight screwtop jar in the refrigerator. Add sufficient Harissa to enhance the flavour of the soup, stirring in a little at a time.

CROUTONS

Discard the crusts from 3–4 slices of white or brown bread. Combine 2–3 tablespoons olive oil and 1–2 peeled, crushed cloves of garlic in a small bowl, then use to brush both sides of the bread. Cut the bread into small cubes and put them on an oven tray. Bake in a preheated 180°C (350°F/Gas 4) oven for 10–15 minutes, or until golden. Allow to cool before serving on top of soups.

Variations: Omit the garlic or add 1/2–1 teaspoon of any ground spice to the oil for an alternative flavour. Croutons can also be made without using any oil. Simply toast the bread cubes in the oven until golden.

SOUPS

PIE-CRUST MUSHROOM SOUP

Preparation time: 25 minutes
Total cooking time: 35 minutes
Serves 4

400 g (14 oz) field mushrooms
60 g (2¼ oz) butter
1 small onion, finely chopped
1 garlic clove, crushed
30 g (¼ cup) plain (all-purpose) flour
750 ml (3 cups) chicken stock
2 tablespoons fresh thyme leaves
2 tablespoons sherry
250 ml (1 cup) cream
1 sheet frozen puff pastry, thawed
1 egg, lightly beaten

1 Preheat the oven to 200°C (400°F/ Gas 6). Roughly chop the mushrooms. Melt the butter in a pan and cook the onion for 3 minutes, until soft. Add the garlic; cook for 1 minute. Add the mushrooms; cook until soft. Sprinkle with the flour and stir for 1 minute.
2 Stir in the stock, add the thyme and bring to the boil. Reduce the heat, cover and simmer for 10 minutes. Cool and process in batches. Return to the pan, stir in the sherry and cream and pour into four ovenproof bowls.
3 Cut rounds of pastry slightly larger than the bowl tops and cover each bowl with pastry (use small deep bowls rather than wide shallow ones or the pastry may sag into the soup).
4 Seal the pastry edges and brush lightly with the beaten egg. Bake for 15 minutes, until golden and puffed.

NUTRITION PER SERVE
Protein 15 g; Fat 50 g; Carbohydrate 25 g; Dietary Fibre 4 g; Cholesterol 180 mg; 2517 kJ (600 Cal)

Stir gently as you sprinkle the flour over the mushrooms in the pan.

Stir in the sherry and cream after you have processed the soup.

Use a lid or cutter to cut pastry rounds a little larger than the bowls.

Seal the edges of the pastry and brush lightly with beaten egg.

PEA AND HAM SOUP

Preparation time: 20 minutes
+ soaking
Total cooking time: 1 hour 30 minutes
Serves 8–10

500 g (1 lb 2 oz) packet green split peas
1 kg (2 lb 4 oz) ham hock or bacon bones, chopped into short pieces (ask your butcher to do this)
2 litres (8 cups) water
1 large onion, chopped
1 large carrot, chopped
1 stick celery, chopped
1 turnip or swede (rutabaga), peeled and chopped
1 parsnip, peeled and chopped
15 g (1/4 cup) chopped fresh parsley

1 Leave the peas to soak overnight or for a minimum of 4 hours in a large bowl of water. Drain, discarding the soaking water.
2 Put the hock or bones in a large heavy-based pan and add the water, peas, onion, carrot, celery, turnip or swede and parsnip. Bring slowly to the boil, reduce the heat and partially cover, then simmer for 1 1/2 hours, or until the peas are reduced to a mush. Stir occasionally, and skim the surface regularly (with a spoon or paper towel) to remove any froth. Remove the pan from the heat and allow to cool a little.
3 Lift out the hock or bones with a pair of tongs or a slotted spoon. Leave them to cool a little before removing the meat. Discard the bones, dice the meat and set aside.
4 When the soup has cooled, purée it in small batches in a food processor or blender. Return the soup to the pan and add the diced meat. Stir in the parsley and re-heat gently to serve.

NUTRITION PER SERVE (10)
Protein 12 g; Fat 1 g; Carbohydrate 26 g; Dietary Fibre 6.5 g; Cholesterol 0 mg; 685 kJ (164 Cal)

COOK'S FILE

Hint: Ham Hock will yield a larger amount of meat than bacon bones, however bacon bones have a more intense flavour.

Peel and chop the parsnip. Ask your butcher to chop the ham hock for you.

Simmer for 1 1/2 hours until the peas are reduced to a mush.

Lift out the ham hock or bacon bones with a pair of tongs.

Return the chopped meat to the soup once it has been puréed.

SMOKED FISH CHOWDER

Preparation time: 20 minutes
Total cooking time: 30–35 minutes
Serves 4–6

500 g (1 lb 2 oz) smoked fish
1 large potato, peeled and diced
1 stick celery, diced
1 medium onion, finely chopped
50 g (1¾ oz) butter
1 rasher bacon, rind removed and finely chopped
2 tablespoons plain (all-purpose) flour
½ teaspoon Worcestershire sauce
½ teaspoon dried mustard
250 ml (1 cup) milk
30 g (½ cup) chopped fresh parsley
60 ml (¼ cup) cream, optional

1 Put the fish in a frying pan, cover with water and bring to the boil, then reduce the heat and simmer for 8 minutes, until the fish flakes easily. Drain, reserving the fish stock, then peel, bone and flake the fish. Set aside.
2 Put the potato, celery and onion in a pan with enough reserved stock to cover the vegetables. Bring to the boil, reduce the heat and simmer for 8 minutes, or until tender. Set aside.
3 Melt the butter in a pan, add the bacon and cook, stirring, for 3 minutes. Add the flour, Worcestershire sauce and mustard and stir until smooth. Cook for 1 minute, gradually pour in the milk and stir, off the heat, until smooth. Return to the heat and stir for 5 minutes until smooth and thick. Stir in the vegetables and liquid, then add the parsley and fish. Simmer over low heat for 5 minutes to heat through. Add the cream, if using.

NUTRITION PER SERVE (6)
Protein 20 g; Fat 14 g; Carbohydrate 9.5 g; Dietary Fibre 1 g; Cholesterol 85 mg; 1020 kJ (245 Cal)

COOK'S FILE

Storage time: Can be kept covered and refrigerated for up to 3 days.

After simmering the fish, use a fork to test if it flakes easily.

Once the fish has been peeled and boned use two forks to flake the flesh.

Add the parsley and flaked fish to the soup once it has thickened.

MULLIGATAWNY SOUP

Preparation time: 20 minutes
Total cooking time: 1 hour 15 minutes
Serves 4

30 g (1 oz) butter
375 g (13 oz) chicken thigh cutlets, skin and fat removed
1 large onion, finely chopped
1 apple, peeled, cored and diced
1 tablespoon curry paste
2 tablespoons plain (all-purpose) flour
750 ml (3 cups) chicken stock
50 g (1/4 cup) basmati rice
1 tablespoon chutney
1 tablespoon lemon juice
60 ml (1/4 cup) cream

1 Heat the butter in a large heavy-based pan and brown the chicken for 5 minutes; remove and set aside. Add the onion, apple and curry paste to the pan. Cook for 5 minutes, until the onion is soft. Stir in the flour; cook for 2 minutes then add half the stock. Stir until the mixture boils and thickens.
2 Return the chicken to the pan with the remaining stock. Stir until boiling, reduce the heat, cover and simmer for 1 hour. Add the rice for the last 15 minutes of cooking.
3 Remove the chicken; bone and dice the meat and return to the pan. Add the chutney, juice and cream. Season.

NUTRITION PER SERVE
Protein 25 g; Fat 16 g; Carbohydrate 25 g; Dietary Fibre 2 g; Cholesterol 28 mg; 1396 kJ (333 Cal)

COOK'S FILE

Storage time: May be kept covered and refrigerated for up to 3 days.

Once the mixture has thickened, return the browned chicken thighs to the pan.

Add the basmati rice during the last 15 minutes of cooking.

Add the chutney, lemon juice and cream at the end of cooking.

HOT BEEF BORSCHT

Preparation time: 30 minutes
Total cooking time: 2 hours
Serves 4–6

500 g (1 lb 2 oz) shin of beef, cut into large pieces
500 g (1 lb 2 oz) fresh beetroot
1 onion, finely chopped
1 carrot, cut into short strips
1 parsnip, cut into short strips
75 g (1 cup) finely shredded cabbage

1 Put the meat in a large heavy-based pan with 1 litre (4 cups) water and bring slowly to the boil; reduce the heat, cover and simmer for 1 hour. Skim the surface frequently to get rid of any froth.

2 Cut away the stems from the beetroot and place it in a large heavy-based pan with 1 litre (4 cups) water. Bring slowly to the boil, reduce the heat and simmer for 40 minutes, or until tender when pierced with a skewer. Drain, reserving the cooking liquid, leave the beetroot to cool, then peel and grate.

3 Use tongs to remove the meat from the stock, leave to cool and dice. Skim any fat from the stock. Return the meat to the stock and add the onion, carrot, parsnip and grated beetroot. Add 250 ml (1 cup) of the beetroot liquid. Bring to the boil, reduce the heat, cover and simmer for 45 minutes. Add more beetroot liquid if a less thick soup is required.

4 Add the cabbage, stir and simmer for a further 15 minutes. Season to taste and serve hot. Borscht is a hearty main-meal soup and is good served with sour cream and chives.

NUTRITION PER SERVE (6)
Protein 22 g; Fat 2.5 g; Carbohydrate 11 g; Dietary Fibre 4 g; Cholesterol 55 mg; 645 kJ (154 Cal)

Cut the parsnip into even-sized strips, each about 4 cm (1 1/2 inch) long.

Use a sharp knife to cut the stems from the beetroot.

You will need to let the beetroot cool before it can be peeled and grated.

Use a pair of tongs to lift the pieces of meat from the stock.

COOK'S FILE

Storage time: May be kept covered and refrigerated for up to 4 days. Suitable to freeze up to 1 month.

PUMPKIN SOUP

Preparation time: 30 minutes
Total cooking time: 50 minutes
Serves 6–8

4–5 kg (9 lb–11 lb 9 oz) whole pumpkin, with 5 cm (2 inch) stem
30 g (1 oz) butter
1 onion, chopped
1 carrot, peeled and chopped
1 teaspoon ground cumin
1/2 teaspoon ground nutmeg
1 teaspoon soft brown sugar
750 ml (3 cups) chicken stock
125 ml (1/2 cup) cream
cream and fresh chives, to serve

1 Preheat the oven to 160°C (315°F/Gas 2–3). Use a small sharp knife to cut a circle from the top of the pumpkin. Scrape the seeds from inside the pumpkin and lid and discard. Scoop out the flesh with a spoon, leaving a thick border. Dice the flesh (you will have about 800 g/1 lb 12 oz) and wash and dry the inside and outside of the pumpkin.

2 Heat the butter in a large heavy-based pan. Add the onion, pumpkin flesh and carrot, cover and cook over low heat for 10 minutes, stirring occasionally. Add the cumin, nutmeg and sugar and cook for 5 minutes more.

3 Add the chicken stock and bring to the boil, reduce the heat and cover. Simmer for 30 minutes, stirring occasionally. Meanwhile, put the pumpkin shell, with its lid on, in the oven for 30 minutes to heat through.

4 Purée the soup, in batches, and return to the clean pan. Season to taste and stir in the cream. Reheat gently without boiling. Ladle into the pumpkin shell, garnish with cream and chives, replace the lid and serve.

NUTRITION PER SERVE (8)
Protein 14 g; Fat 12 g; Carbohydrate 45 g; Dietary Fibre 8 g; Cholesterol 30 mg; 1410 kJ (336 Cal)

COOK'S FILE

Storage time: May be kept covered and refrigerated (not in the shell) for up to 3 days. Freeze for up to 1 month.

Cut a circle from the top of the pumpkin using a small sharp knife.

Use paper towels to dry the pumpkin shell inside and out.

Add the cumin, nutmeg and sugar and cook for a further 5 minutes.

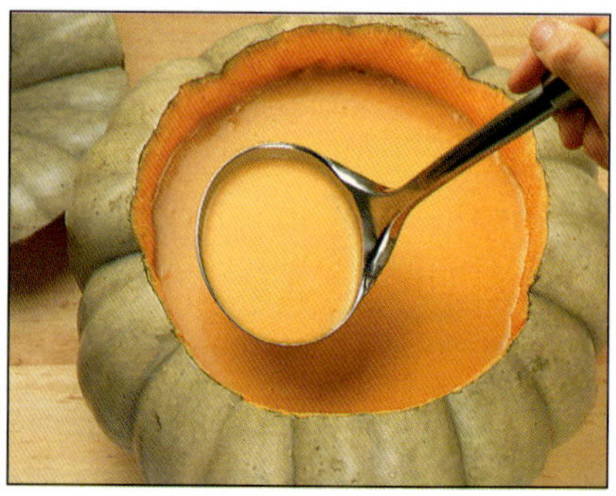

Carefully ladle the soup into the warmed pumpkin shell to serve.

SCOTCH BROTH

Preparation time: 20 minutes
Total cooking time: 2 hours 30 minutes
Serves 8–10

750 g (1 lb 10 oz) best neck of lamb chops or lamb shanks
250 g (9 oz) pearl barley or soup mix
1 carrot, peeled and diced
1 turnip, peeled and diced
1 parsnip, peeled and diced
1 onion, finely chopped
1 small leek, thinly sliced
75 g (1 cup) finely chopped cabbage
30 g (½ cup) chopped parsley

1 Cut away any excess fat from the meat; place the meat in a large heavy-based pan with 2.5 litres (10 cups) water. Bring to the boil, reduce the heat and simmer, covered, for 1 hour. Skim any froth from the surface. Meanwhile, soak the barley or soup mix in a bowl of water for 1 hour.

2 Add the carrot, turnip, parsnip, onion and leek to the pan. Drain the barley and add to the pan. Stir to combine, cover and simmer for 1½ hours. Stir in the cabbage 10 minutes before the end of cooking time. (Add more water, according to taste.)

3 Remove the meat from the pan, and cool before removing from the bones. Chop the meat finely and return to the soup. Add the parsley and season.

NUTRITION PER SERVE (10)
Protein 21 g; Fat 2 g; Carbohydrate 20 g; Dietary Fibre 4 g; Cholesterol 50 mg; 750 kJ (180 Cal)

COOK'S FILE

Storage time: May be kept covered and refrigerated for up to 3 days. Suitable to freeze up to 1 month.

Note: Soup mix is a combination of pearl barley, split peas and lentils.

Instead of a spoon, use paper towels to skim any froth from the surface.

Drain the barley or soup mix and add to the pan.

Use tongs to hold the bones while removing the meat.

MEDITERRANEAN FISH SOUP

Preparation time: 25 minutes
Total cooking time: 25 minutes
Serves 6–8

1 kg (2 lb 4 oz) white fish fillets
60 ml (1/4 cup) olive oil
2 large onions, chopped
1–2 garlic cloves, crushed
4 large tomatoes, peeled, seeded and chopped
2 tablespoons tomato paste (purée)
6 tablespoons chopped gherkins
1 tablespoon chopped capers
1 tablespoon pitted and chopped green olives
1 tablespoon pitted and chopped black olives
750 ml (3 cups) fish stock
250 ml (1 cup) white wine
1 bay leaf
15 g (1/4 cup) chopped fresh basil
60 g (1 cup) chopped fresh parsley

1 Remove the skin and bones from the fish and chop into bite-sized pieces. Heat the oil in a large heavy-based pan and cook the onion and garlic for 8 minutes until soft.

2 Stir in the tomato and paste. Stir for 2–3 minutes, or until the tomato is soft. Stir in the gherkins and half the capers and olives.

3 Add the fish, stock, wine and bay leaf and season. Bring slowly to the boil, reduce the heat and simmer for 10–12 minutes, or until the fish is just cooked. Stir in the herbs. Add the remaining capers and olives. Serve.

NUTRITION PER SERVE (8)
Protein 20 g; Fat 11 g; Carbohydrate 7 g; Dietary Fibre 2.5 g; Cholesterol 88 mg; 1101 kJ (263 Cal)

COOK'S FILE

Note: Unsuitable to freeze.

Peel the tomatoes by soaking in boiling water. Remove the seeds with a spoon.

Use salt to help you keep a firm grasp on the fish while removing the skin.

Add the fish to the pan and pour in the stock and white wine.

SPICY LAMB SOUP

Preparation time: 40 minutes
Total cooking time: 1 hour 30 minutes
Serves 4–6

2 large onions, roughly chopped
3 red chillies, seeded, chopped (or 2 teaspoons dried chilli)
3–4 garlic cloves
2 cm (3/4 inch) piece ginger, chopped
1 teaspoon ground black pepper
6 cm (2 1/2 inch) piece lemon grass, white only, chopped
1/2 teaspoon ground cardamom
2 teaspoons ground cumin
1/2 teaspoon ground cinnamon
1 teaspoon ground turmeric
2 tablespoons peanut oil
1.5 kg (3 lb 5 oz) lamb neck chops
2–3 tablespoons vindaloo paste
580 ml (2 1/3 cups) coconut cream
45 g (1/4 cup) soft brown sugar
2–3 tablespoons lime juice
4 makrut (kaffir) lime leaves

1 Put the onion, chilli, garlic, ginger, pepper, lemon grass and spices in a food processor. Process to a paste. Heat half the oil in a large pan and brown the chops in batches. Remove.

2 Add the remaining oil to the pan and cook the spice and vindaloo pastes for 2–3 minutes. Add the chops and 1.75 litres (7 cups) water, cover and bring to the boil. Reduce the heat; simmer, covered, for 1 hour. Remove the chops from the pan and stir in the coconut cream. Remove the meat from the bones, shred and return to the pan.

3 Add the sugar, lime juice and leaves. Simmer, uncovered, over low heat for 20–25 minutes, until slightly thickened. Garnish with coriander (cilantro).

NUTRITION PER SERVE (6)
Protein 55 g; Fat 38 g; Carbohydrate 17 g; Dietary Fibre 3 g; Cholesterol 166 mg; 2602 kJ (622 Cal)

Wear disposable gloves when working with chillies to avoid smarting and burns.

Process the onions with the chilli, garlic and spices to make a paste.

Trim away any excess fat from the chops before cooking.

CARROT AND ORANGE SOUP

Preparation time: 20 minutes
Total cooking time: 30 minutes
Serves 4

60 g (2¼ oz) butter
500 g (1 lb 2 oz) carrots, peeled and sliced
1 large onion, thinly sliced
1–2 teaspoons grated orange zest
1 tablespoon plain (all-purpose) flour
125 ml (½ cup) fresh orange juice
1.25 litres (5 cups) chicken stock
185 ml (¾ cup) cream
chives and orange zest, to serve

1 Heat the butter in a large pan and add the carrot, onion and orange zest; stir over low heat until the onion is softened and translucent.
2 Stir in the flour. Gradually add the juice and stock, stirring until combined. Stir over heat until the mixture boils and thickens. Reduce the heat, cover and simmer over low heat for 25 minutes, or until the carrot is tender.
3 Cool slightly before processing in batches until smooth. Return to the pan, stir in the cream and season. Stir over gentle heat until warmed through—do not boil. Garnish with chives and orange zest.

NUTRITION PER SERVE
Protein 4 g; Fat 33 g; Carbohydrate 16 g; Dietary Fibre 5 g; Cholesterol 100 mg; 1533 kJ (366 Cal)

When grating oranges only grate the zest, not the bitter white pith.

Add the juice and stock gradually and stir to prevent lumps forming.

Allow the soup to cool a little before processing to avoid hot soup splashing.

CHICKEN AND SWEETCORN SOUP

Preparation time: 25 minutes
Total cooking time: 20 minutes
Serves 4–6

2 corn cobs
1.5 litres (6 cups) chicken stock
235 g (1⅓ cups) shredded cooked chicken
2 cm (¾ inch) piece fresh ginger, peeled and finely grated
2 tablespoons cornflour (cornstarch)
440 g (16 oz) can creamed corn
8 spring onions (scallions), finely chopped
½ teaspoon sesame oil

1 Steam the corn cobs until tender (about 10–15 minutes). Cool until they are easily handled, then cut the kernels from the cobs. Discard the cobs.
2 Heat the stock in a heavy-based pan and add the corn, chicken and ginger. Reduce the heat and simmer, uncovered, for 5 minutes.
3 Blend the cornflour and 80 ml (⅓ cup) water until smooth. Add to the pan, stirring continuously, and stir over medium heat until the soup boils and thickens slightly. Reduce the heat, add the creamed corn, spring onion and oil and stir gently to combine. Season, leave to simmer for 2 minutes and serve immediately.

NUTRITION PER SERVE (6)
Protein 9 g; Fat 3 g; Carbohydrate 20 g; Dietary Fibre 4 g; Cholesterol 18 mg; 611 kJ (145 Cal)

COOK'S FILE

Variation: Fresh corn adds texture and a distinctive taste but if it isn't available, use a drained can of corn kernels instead.

Once the corn is cooked it should be easy to cut the kernels from the cobs.

Add the corn, chicken and ginger to the stock in the pan.

Add the creamed corn and spring onion when the soup has thickened a little.

Carrot and Orange Soup (top) and Chicken and Sweetcorn Soup

BOUILLABAISSE

Preparation time: 40 minutes
Total cooking time: 1 hour 30 minutes
Serves 4–6

500 g (1 lb 2 oz) raw king prawns (shrimp)
1 lobster tail
1–2 fish heads
250 ml (1 cup) red wine
1 small and 2 medium red onions, finely chopped
6 garlic cloves, crushed
3 bay leaves
60 ml (1/4 cup) olive oil
1 small leek, finely sliced
4–6 ripe tomatoes, peeled and chopped
60 g (1/4 cup) tomato paste (purée)
5 cm (2 inch) piece orange zest
500 g (1 lb 2 oz) white fish, skinned and boned, cut into 3 cm (1 1/4 inch) pieces
12 mussels, beards removed
200 g (7 oz) scallops with corals
30 g (1/2 cup) chopped parsley
15 g (1/4 cup) shredded basil leaves

1 Peel and devein the prawns, reserving the heads and tails. Shell the lobster tail, keeping the shell and chopping the meat. Put the fish heads, prawn shells, heads and tails and the lobster shell in a large pan. Add the wine, small onion, 2 garlic cloves, 1 bay leaf and 500 ml (2 cups) water. Bring to the boil, then reduce the heat and simmer for 20 minutes. Strain, reserving the liquid.

2 Heat the oil in a large heavy-based pan. Add the leek and remaining onion and garlic. Cover and simmer, stirring occasionally, over low heat for 20 minutes, or until browned. Add the tomato, paste, remaining bay leaves and zest, stir well and season. Uncover and cook for 10 minutes, stirring often. Add the reserved fish stock, bring to the boil and keep boiling for 10 minutes, stirring often.

3 Reduce the heat, add the seafood and simmer, covered, for 4–5 minutes. Discard any mussels which haven't opened. Remove the zest and the bay leaves. Sprinkle with the herbs to serve.

NUTRITION PER SERVE (6)
Protein 44 g; Fat 13 g; Carbohydrate 7 g; Dietary Fibre 4 g; Cholesterol 210 mg; 1475 kJ (350 Cal)

Remove the large black veins from the backs of the prawns.

Pull away the beards from the mussels and discard any which are already open.

You need to be firm to pull the shell away from the lobster tail.

Cook the onions slowly until they are tender and deep golden.

Grill the slices of French bread for 2–3 minutes, turning once.

Spread the cheese mixture over the slices of French bread.

Grill until the cheese has just melted and serve immediately with the soup.

FRENCH ONION SOUP WITH CAMEMBERT EN CROUTE

Preparation time: 25 minutes
Total cooking time: 1 hour 15 minutes
Serves 4–6

6 onions (about 1 kg/2 lb 4 oz)
60 g (2 1/4 oz) butter
1 teaspoon soft brown sugar
30 g (1/4 cup) plain (all-purpose) flour
2.25 litres (9 cups) beef stock
1/2 stick French bread
1–2 garlic cloves, crushed
2 tablespoons grated Cheddar cheese
125 g (4 1/2 oz) camembert cheese, chopped
1 tablespoon chopped fresh parsley

1 Peel the onions and slice into fine rings. Heat the butter in a large heavy-based pan, add the onion and sugar and cook slowly over low heat for about 30 minutes, or until the onion is very tender and deep golden. Add the flour and cook, stirring, for 1–2 minutes, or until the flour starts to turn golden.

2 Stir in the stock, cover and simmer over low heat for 1 hour. Season well.

3 Slice the bread thinly and grill (broil) for 2–3 minutes, turning once, until lightly golden. Mash the garlic, cheeses and parsley with a fork, spread over the bread and grill until the cheese has just melted.

4 Pour the soup into bowls and top with the bread, cheese-side-up.

NUTRITION PER SERVE (6)
Protein 10 g; Fat 17 g; Carbohydrate 20 g; Dietary Fibre 3 g; Cholesterol 50 mg; 1095 kJ (260 Cal)

COOK'S FILE

Variation: For a richer soup replace 250–500 ml (1–2 cups) of the beef stock with a good red wine.

NORWEGIAN FISH SOUP

Preparation time: 20 minutes
Total cooking time: 25 minutes
Serve 4–6

30 g (1 oz) butter
2 carrots, diced
1 parsnip, peeled and diced
1 medium leek, white part only, sliced
1 teaspoon celery seeds
500 g (1 lb 2 oz) skinned and boneless white fish fillets
500 ml (2 cups) milk
185 ml (3/4 cup) white wine
2 teaspoons cornflour (cornstarch)
1 tablespoon milk, extra
2 egg yolks
125 g (1/2 cup) sour cream
30 g (1/2 cup) chopped fresh parsley

1 Heat the butter in a large heavy-based pan, add the vegetables and celery seeds and stir over medium heat for 3 minutes, without allowing the vegetables to brown. Chop the fish into bite-sized pieces and add to the vegetables in the pan.
2 Stir in the milk and wine. Bring to the boil, reduce the heat and simmer for 15 minutes. Remove from the heat.
3 Blend the cornflour and extra milk and mix together with the egg yolks and sour cream. Add to the pan, reduce the heat and stir continuously for 3–5 minutes, or until the soup thickens a little, but doesn't boil. Stir in the parsley and season to taste.

NUTRITION PER SERVE (6)
Protein 20 g; Fat 16g; Carbohydrate 10 g; Dietary Fibre 3 g; Cholesterol 155 mg; 1201 kJ (285 Cal)

COOK'S FILE

Storage time: The soup is best served immediately, but will keep, covered and refrigerated for up to a day. It is unsuitable to freeze.

Variations: Replace the wine and/or some of the milk with fish stock. Use cream instead of sour cream. For a less chunky soup, finely chop the vegetables in a food processor.

Stir the vegetables and celery seeds over medium heat.

Stir in the milk and white wine and bring to the boil.

Mix the blended cornflour and milk with the egg yolks and sour cream.

CREAM OF TOMATO SOUP

Preparation time: 15 minutes
Total cooking time: 25 minutes
Serves 4

1 tablespoon olive oil
1 onion, chopped
2 garlic cloves, crushed
1.2 kg (2 lb 10 oz) canned crushed tomatoes
750 ml (3 cups) chicken stock
1 tablespoon tomato paste (purée)
2 teaspoons soft brown sugar
250 ml (1 cup) cream

1 Heat the oil in a heavy-based pan. Add the onion and cook for 5 minutes over medium heat until soft but not brown. Add the garlic and cook for a further minute.
2 Add the tomatoes to the pan, with the stock, tomato paste and sugar. Season. Bring to the boil, reduce the heat and simmer, partially covered, for 20 minutes.
3 Cool slightly and purée in batches until smooth. Return to the pan, add the cream and reheat gently.

NUTRITION PER SERVE
Protein 5 g; Fat 30 g; Carbohydrate 15 g; Dietary Fibre 5 g; Cholesterol 85 mg; 1518 kJ (365 Cal)

COOK'S FILE

Note: If available, use good, fresh tomatoes. Use 1 kg (2 lb 4 oz) ripe tomatoes and 1 litre (4 cups) chicken stock. Peel the tomatoes by plunging them first in boiling water then cold.

Cook the onion until softened and translucent but not brown.

Add the crushed tomatoes with the stock and tomato paste.

Reheat gently after stirring in the cream, but do not boil.

STILTON AND APPLE SOUP

Preparation time: 20 minutes
Total cooking time: 30 minutes
Serves 8

40 g (1½ oz) butter
2 tablespoons plain (all-purpose) flour
750 ml (3 cups) chicken stock
4 red apples
500 ml (2 cups) milk
250 g (9 oz) Stilton cheese
2 tablespoons chopped chives

1 Melt the butter in a large heavy-based pan. Sprinkle with the flour and stir over low heat for 2 minutes, or until lightly golden. Gradually add the stock, stirring until smooth.

2 Peel, core and slice the apples and add to the pan. Cook, covered, over medium heat for 20 minutes, or until tender. Cool, then purée in a processor in batches until smooth.

3 Return the soup to the pan, add the milk and reheat, stirring. Simmer gently and add the crumbled Stilton and chives. Stir until the soup is smooth and serve immediately.

NUTRITION PER SERVE
Protein 9 g; Fat 17 g; Carbohydrate 15 g; Dietary Fibre 2 g; Cholesterol 50 mg; 1020 kJ (245 Cal)

Add the stock gradually, stirring all the time to prevent lumps forming.

To test if the apples are tender insert the tip of a sharp knife.

Add the crumbled Stilton while the soup simmers and stir until smooth.

MINESTRONE

Preparation time: 30 minutes + overnight soaking
Total cooking time: 2 hours 45 minutes
Serves 6–8

250 g (9 oz) dried borlotti beans
2 tablespoons oil
2 onions, chopped
2 garlic cloves, crushed
80 g (1/2 cup) chopped bacon pieces
4 Roma (plum) tomatoes, peeled and chopped
15 g (1/4 cup) chopped fresh parsley
2.25 litres (9 cups) beef stock
60 ml (1/4 cup) red wine
1 carrot, peeled and chopped
1 swede (rutabaga), peeled and diced
2 potatoes, peeled and diced
3 tablespoons tomato paste (purée)
2 zucchini (courgettes), sliced
80 g (1/2 cup) green peas, shelled
80 g (1/2 cup) small macaroni
Parmesan and pesto, to serve

1 Soak the borlotti beans in water overnight and drain. Add to a pan of boiling water, simmer for 15 minutes and drain. Heat the oil in a large heavy-based pan and cook the onion, garlic and bacon pieces, stirring, until the onion is soft and the bacon golden.

2 Add the tomato, parsley, borlotti beans, stock and red wine. Simmer, covered, over low heat for 2 hours. Add the carrot, swede, potato and tomato paste, cover and simmer for 15–20 minutes.

3 Add the zucchini, peas and pasta. Cover and simmer for 10–15 minutes, or until the vegetables and macaroni are tender. Season to taste and serve topped with grated Parmesan and a little pesto.

NUTRITION PER SERVE (8)
Protein 15 g; Fat 7 g; Carbohydrate 25 g; Dietary Fibre 10 g; Cholesterol 12 mg; 955 kJ (228 Cal)

Soak the borlotti beans in a bowl of water overnight and then drain.

Use a sharp knife to peel and dice the swede and other vegetables.

Stir the onion and bacon over the heat until soft and golden.

LENTIL AND VEGETABLE SOUP

Preparation time: 30 minutes + 2 hours soaking
Total cooking time: 1 hour
Serves 8–10

280 g ($1\frac{1}{2}$ cups) green lentils
1 tablespoon olive oil
1 onion, finely chopped
1 teaspoon ground paprika
1 teaspoon ground oregano
2 litres (8 cups) vegetable stock
400 g (14 oz) can tomatoes, chopped
3 tablespoons tomato paste (purée)
3 sticks celery, thinly sliced
2 medium carrots, thinly sliced
2 bay leaves
3 small zucchini (courgettes), thinly sliced
150 g ($5\frac{1}{2}$ oz) beans, cut in half

1 Soak the lentils in cold water for 2 hours and then rinse and drain well. Heat the oil in a large heavy-based pan and cook the onion over medium heat until soft but not browned, stirring occasionally (this will take about 3 minutes). Stir in the paprika and oregano and cook for a further minute.

2 Add the lentils, stock, undrained tomatoes and tomato paste to the pan; bring to the boil and then reduce the heat to low and simmer, uncovered, for 5 minutes.

3 Add the celery, carrot and bay leaves and stir well. Bring to the boil, reduce the heat and simmer, covered, for 40 minutes until thickened.

4 Add the zucchini and beans and leave to simmer, covered, for a further 10–15 minutes, or until the vegetables are tender. Remove the bay leaves before serving with crusty bread.

NUTRITION PER SERVE (10)
Protein 11 g; Fat 3 g; Carbohydrate 18 g; Dietary Fibre 8 g; Cholesterol 0 mg; 590 kJ (140 Cal)

Soak and rinse the lentils well and pick out any which are discoloured.

Add the celery, carrot and bay leaves before bringing to the boil again.

Leave the soup to simmer, covered, for 40 minutes until it has thickened.

CREAM OF CHICKEN SOUP

Preparation time: 15 minutes
Total cooking time: 20 minutes
Serves 4–6

60 g ($2\frac{1}{4}$ oz) butter
40 g ($\frac{1}{3}$ cup) plain (all-purpose) flour
750 ml (3 cups) chicken stock
250 ml (1 cup) milk
2 chicken breast fillets, sliced
250 ml (1 cup) cream
1 stick celery, finely sliced
7 g ($\frac{1}{4}$ cup) lemon thyme leaves
2 spring onions (scallions), finely sliced

1 Melt the butter in a large pan and add the flour. Stir over low heat for 2 minutes, or until lightly golden.

2 Gradually add the stock, stirring between each addition until smooth. Stir continuously over moderate heat until the mixture boils and thickens.

3 Reduce the heat and add the milk, chicken, cream and celery. Simmer over low for 5 minutes, until chicken is cooked but tender. Season. Sprinkle with thyme and spring onions. Serve.

NUTRITION PER SERVE (6)
Protein 13 g; Fat 30 g; Carbohydrate 15 g; Dietary Fibre 0.5 g; Cholesterol 108 mg; 1519 kJ (365 Cal)

Stir the flour and butter over low heat until lightly golden.

Once you have added the stock, stir until the mixture boils and thickens.

Reduce the heat and then add the milk, chicken, cream and celery.

Lentil and Vegetable Soup (top) and Cream of Chicken Soup

SWEET CORN
SUGAR PEAS
CUT RED BEETS
DEFENDER
PEAS
WINSOM
DICED CARROTS
SMALL WHOLE BEETS

CREAMY BEETROOT SOUP

Preparation time: 15 minutes
Total cooking time: 50 minutes
Serves 6

1 tablespoon oil
1 small onion, chopped
1.5 kg (3 lb 5 oz) beetroot, peeled, chopped
1.25 litres (5 cups) vegetable stock
2 teaspoons caraway seeds
2 tablespoons horseradish cream
250 g (9 oz) sour cream

1 Heat the oil in a heavy-based pan. Cook the onion over medium heat for 5 minutes until soft.

2 Add the beetroot, stock and seeds; bring to the boil. Simmer, partially covered, for 40 minutes.

3 Cool, then process in batches until smooth. Reheat gently and stir in the horseradish and sour cream to serve.

NUTRITION PER SERVE
Protein 6 g; Fat 20 g; Carbohydrate 23 g; Dietary Fibre 8 g; Cholesterol 55 mg; 1245 kJ (295 Cal)

COOK'S FILE

Storage time: Can be kept in the fridge for 1 day. Add the sour cream and horseradish when you reheat.

Peel the beetroot with a potato peeler before dicing the flesh.

Add the beetroot, stock and caraway seeds and bring to the boil.

Stir in the horseradish and sour cream after processing the soup.

CHICKEN NOODLE SOUP

Preparation time: 20 minutes
Total cooking time: 20–25 minutes
Serves 4–6

2.25 litres (9 cups) chicken stock
175 g (6 oz) shredded cooked chicken
100 g (3 1/2 oz) broken thin noodles
15 g (1/4 cup) chopped fresh chives
45 g (3/4 cup) chopped fresh parsley

1 Put the stock in a pan and bring to the boil. Add the shredded chicken.
2 Add the noodles, chives and parsley to the pan and simmer over low heat for 15–20 minutes, or until the noodles are tender. Season, then spoon into bowls. Serve immediately.

NUTRITION PER SERVE
Protein 45 g; Fat 8 g; Carbohydrate 8 g; Dietary Fibre 2 g; Cholesterol 135 mg; 1205 kJ (290 Cal)

COOK'S FILE

Hints: The noodles must be added immediately before serving, otherwise they will soften too much and become soggy if left to stand.

- If real chicken stock is unavailable, use 2 litres (8 cups) water with 1 tablespoon chicken stock powder.

To finely shred the cooked chicken pull it apart with two forks.

Add the thin noodles to the pan of stock and shredded chicken.

Simmer until the chicken is cooked and the noodles tender.

WHOLE GREEN PEA SOUP

Preparation time: 20 minutes + 1 hour soaking
Total cooking time: 40 minutes
Serves 6

1 kg (2 lb 4 oz) green peas in the pod
1 litre (4 cups) vegetable stock
30 g (1 oz) butter
1 small onion, sliced
2 tablespoons finely chopped flat-leaf (Italian) parsley
2 tablespoons olive oil
4 thick slices bread, cut into 1 cm (1/2 inch) cubes

1 Shell the peas and set them aside. Cut the stringy tops from the pods and discard them. Wash the pods thoroughly and place in a large bowl. Cover with cold water and leave to stand for 1 hour. Drain the pods well and put them in a large heavy-based pan. Add the stock and bring to the boil, reduce the heat and simmer, covered, for 15 minutes, or until the pods are tender. Leave to cool slightly.
2 Put the pods and stock in batches into a food processor or blender and process for 30 seconds until smooth. Strain the purée, discarding the pods.
3 Melt the butter in a pan, add the onion and cook over medium heat until soft. Add the peas, parsley and 250 ml (1 cup) of water, bring to the boil, reduce the heat to low and cook, covered, for 15 minutes until tender.
4 Heat the oil in a frying pan, add the bread cubes and cook until lightly brown. Remove them from the pan and leave to drain on paper towels.
5 Add the purée of pea pods to the simmering peas and stir through. Bring to the boil, reduce the heat and simmer for 5 minutes to heat through. Season and serve with the croutons.

NUTRITION PER SERVE
Protein 12 g; Fat 12 g; Carbohydrate 23 g; Dietary Fibre 10 g; Cholesterol 23 mg; 1019 kJ (243 Cal)

COOK'S FILE

Variation: Add 125 ml (1/2 cup) of cream at the end and heat through.
Hint: If the pea pods seem quite tough remove the tails as well as tops.

Shell the peas and set them aside but keep the pods.

Simmer the pods in stock for 15 minutes until they are tender.

Fry the bread cubes in hot oil until lightly brown and then drain on paper towels.

Add the strained purée of pea pods to the simmering peas.

ROASTED RED CAPSICUM SOUP

Preparation time: 50 minutes
Total cooking time: 1 hour
Serves 6

4 large red capsicums (peppers)
4 medium ripe tomatoes
2 tablespoons oil
1 red onion, chopped
1 garlic clove, crushed
1 litre (4 cups) vegetable stock
1 teaspoon sweet chilli sauce
Pesto and Parmesan, to garnish

1 Cut the capsicums into large flat pieces, removing the seeds and membrane. Place skin-side-up under a hot grill (broiler) until blackened. Leave covered with a tea towel until cool. Peel off the skin and chop the flesh.

2 Cut a small cross in the base of each tomato, put in a large heatproof bowl and cover with boiling water. Leave for 1 minute, plunge into cold water and peel the skin from the cross. Cut in half, scoop out the seeds and roughly chop the flesh.

3 Heat the oil in a large heavy-based pan and add the onion. Cook over medium heat for 10 minutes, stirring frequently, until very soft. Add the garlic and cook for a further minute. Add the capsicum, tomato and stock; bring to the boil, reduce the heat and simmer for about 20 minutes.

4 Allow the soup to cool slightly before processing in batches until smooth. Return to the pan to reheat gently and stir in the chilli sauce (vary the amount according to your taste). This soup is delicious topped with pesto and shavings of Parmesan.

NUTRITION PER SERVE
Protein 3 g; Fat 7 g; Carbohydrate 5 g; Dietary Fibre 2 g; Cholesterol 0 mg; 380 kJ (90 Cal)

Once the skin of the capsicum has been blackened it should peel away easily.

Cutting a cross in the base of the tomato makes it easier to remove the skin.

Use a spoon to scoop out the seeds from the tomatoes once they have been peeled.

SPICY CHICKEN BROTH WITH CORIANDER PASTA

Preparation time: 40 minutes
Total cooking time: 50 minutes
Serves 4

350 g (12 oz) chicken thighs or wings, skin removed
2 carrots, finely chopped
2 sticks celery, finely chopped
2 small leeks, finely chopped
3 egg whites
1.5 litres (6 cups) chicken stock
Tabasco sauce

Coriander Pasta
60 g (1/2 cup) plain (all-purpose) flour
1 egg
1/2 teaspoon sesame oil
coriander (cilantro) leaves

1 Put the chicken, carrot, celery and leek in a large heavy-based pan. Push the chicken to one side and add the egg whites to the vegetables. Using a wire whisk, beat for a minute or so until frothy (take care not to use a pan that can be scratched by the whisk).

2 Warm the stock in another pan, then add gradually to the first pan, whisking continuously to froth the egg whites. Continue whisking while slowly bringing to the boil. Make a hole in the froth on top with a spoon and leave to simmer, uncovered, for 30 minutes without stirring.

3 Line a large strainer with a damp tea towel or double thickness of muslin and strain the broth into a clean bowl (discard the chicken and vegetables). Season with salt, pepper and Tabasco to taste. Set aside.

4 To make the Coriander Pasta: sift the flour into a bowl and make a well in the centre. Whisk the egg and oil together and pour into the well. Mix together to make a soft pasta dough and knead on a lightly floured surface for 2 minutes, until smooth.

5 Divide the dough into four even portions. Roll one portion out very thinly and cover with a layer of evenly spaced coriander leaves. Roll out another portion of pasta and lay on top of the leaves, then gently roll the layers together. Repeat with the remaining pasta and coriander.

6 Cut out squares of pasta around the leaves. The pasta may then be left to sit and dry out if it is not needed immediately. When you are ready to serve, heat the chicken broth gently in a saucepan. As the broth simmers, add the pasta and cook for 1 minute. Serve immediately.

NUTRITION PER SERVE
Protein 25 g; Fat 4 g; Carbohydrate 18 g; Dietary Fibre 4 g; Cholesterol 90 mg; 915 kJ (220 Cal)

COOK'S FILE

Hint: Beg, borrow or steal a pasta machine for making this fine, delicate pasta. A rolling pin will suffice if necessary but try to roll the pasta as thinly as possible.

Note: The egg whites added to the vegetable and chicken stock pot make the broth very clear rather than leaving it with the normal cloudy appearance of chicken stock. This is called clarifying the stock. When you strain the broth through muslin or a tea towel, don't press the solids to extract the extra liquid or the broth will become cloudy. It is necessary to make a hole in the froth on top to prevent the stock boiling over.

Use a wire whisk to beat the egg white and vegetables.

Use a metal spoon to make a hole in the froth on top of the soup.

Strain the broth through a damp tea towel or double thickness of muslin.

Knead the dough on a lightly floured surface until it is smooth.

Lay a second layer of thin pasta over the coriander leaves.

Cut out neat squares of pasta around each coriander leaf.

CLAM CHOWDER

Preparation time: 35 minutes
Total cooking time: 40 minutes
Serves 4

1.5 kg (3 lb 5 oz) fresh clams (vongole) in shell
1 tablespoon oil
3 rashers bacon, chopped
1 onion, chopped
1 garlic clove, crushed
4 potatoes, cubed
310 ml (1 1/4 cups) fish stock
500 ml (2 cups) milk
125 ml (1/2 cup) cream
15 g (1/4 cup) chopped fresh parsley

1 Discard any clams which are already open. Put the remainder in a large heavy-based pan with 250 ml (1 cup) water and simmer, covered, over low heat for 5 minutes, or until the shells open (discard any clams which do not open during cooking). Strain the liquid and reserve. Remove the clam meat from the shells, discarding the shells.
2 Heat the oil in a clean pan and then add the bacon, onion and garlic. Cook, stirring, until the onion is soft and the bacon golden. Add the potato and stir to combine.
3 Measure the reserved clam liquid and add enough water to make it up to 310 ml (1 1/4 cups). Add this to the pan with the stock and milk. Bring to the boil and then reduce the heat, cover and simmer for 20 minutes, or until the potato is tender.
4 Uncover and leave to simmer for a further 10 minutes, or until reduced and slightly thickened. Add the cream, clam meat, salt and pepper to taste and parsley. Heat through gently before serving but do not allow to boil or the flavour will be impaired.

NUTRITION PER SERVE
Protein 5 g; Fat 12 g; Carbohydrate 17 g; Dietary Fibre 3 g; Cholesterol 20 mg; 825 kJ (197 Cal)

COOK'S FILE

Variation: Fresh clams, often available at fish markets, give the best flavour but you can use canned. Don't use the brine from the can—drain them before using and make up the liquid with fresh fish stock.

Use your fingers to remove the clam meat from the shells.

Add the potato cubes to the cooked bacon, onion and garlic.

Simmer the chowder for 20 minutes, or until the potato is tender.

Add the cream, clam meat and parsley and then heat through gently.

ROASTED PUMPKIN SOUP

Preparation time: 20 minutes
Total cooking time: 1 hour 35 minutes
Serves 6–8

1 kg (2 lb 4 oz) pumpkin, cut into small chunks, skin on
2 tablespoons olive oil
1 red onion, chopped
2 garlic cloves, crushed
4 potatoes, peeled and cut into 2 cm (3/4 inch) cubes
1.125 litres (4 1/2 cups) vegetable stock
125 ml (1/2 cup) cream
10 fresh basil leaves, shredded

1 Preheat the oven to 180°C (350°F/Gas 4). Put the pumpkin on an oven tray, sprinkle with water and cook for 30–35 minutes, or until tender. Scoop out the flesh, discarding the skin. Mash and set aside.

2 Heat the oil in a heavy-based pan. Add the onion and garlic and cook over medium heat for 4 minutes until soft and lightly browned. Add the roasted pumpkin, potato, and 875 ml (3 1/2 cups) of the stock. Stir well and bring to the boil. Reduce the heat, cover and simmer for 45 minutes, or until the mixture breaks down and thickens. Season to taste.

3 Stir in the remaining stock. Bring to the boil and simmer for 10 minutes, or until the soup reaches the desired consistency. Serve with a swirl of cream and shredded basil leaves.

NUTRITION PER SERVE
Protein 5 g; Fat 12 g; Carbohydrate 17 g; Dietary Fibre 3 g; Cholesterol 20 mg; 825 kJ (197 Cal)

COOK'S FILE

Variation: Try using butternut or little golden nugget pumpkin: either of these will give a sweeter flavour to this recipe.

Cut the pumpkin into chunks and put on an oven tray for roasting.

The roasted flesh should be soft and easy to scoop out with a spoon.

Leave the soup to simmer until the mixture has broken down and thickened.

VICHYSSOISE
(Leek and Potato Soup)

Preparation time: 25 minutes
Total cooking time: 15–20 minutes
Serves 4–6

60 g (2¼ oz) butter
2 leeks, chopped
2 large potatoes, chopped
750 ml (3 cups) chicken stock
250 ml (1 cup) milk
sour cream, for serving
chives, chopped, for serving

1 Heat the butter in a medium pan and cook the leeks until soft.
2 Add the potato and chicken stock and simmer for 15–20 minutes, or until the potato is tender. Stir in the milk and season with salt and freshly ground black pepper.
3 Cool, then blend in batches until smooth. Vichyssoise is traditionally served well-chilled, but if you prefer, return to the pan and reheat gently without boiling. Whether hot or chilled, spoon sour cream on top and sprinkle with chives to serve.

NUTRITION PER SERVE (6)
Protein 2 g; Fat 10 g; Carbohydrate 4 g; Dietary Fibre 1 g; Cholesterol 35 mg; 512 kJ (122 Cal)

COOK'S FILE

Note: Vichyssoise is a classic chilled cream soup created by the Ritz-Carlton Hotel in New York.

Cook the leeks in butter in a medium pan until they are soft.

Once the potato is tender, stir in the milk and then season to taste.

Allow the soup to cool to make it easier and safer to process.

When hard-boiling eggs start them off in cold water to prevent the shells cracking.

To skin the tomatoes leave them in a bowl of boiling water for 2 minutes.

Chop the tomato flesh finely—it is best to do this in 2 batches.

Stir all the soup ingredients together in a large bowl before chilling.

GAZPACHO

Preparation time: 30 minutes
Total cooking time: Nil
Serves 4–6

750 g (1 lb 10 oz) ripe tomatoes
1 Lebanese (short) cucumber, diced
1 large green capsicum (pepper), diced
2–3 garlic cloves, crushed
2 tablespoons diced black olives
60 ml (1/4 cup) olive oil
80 ml (1/3 cup) red or white wine vinegar
1 tablespoon tomato paste (purée)

Accompaniments
1 red onion, diced
1 small red capsicum (pepper), diced
2 spring onions (scallions), finely sliced
2 hard-boiled eggs, chopped
1 Lebanese (short) cucumber, diced
chopped fresh marjoram, mint or parsley
croutons

1 Cut a cross in the base of each tomato and put in a bowl of boiling water. Leave for 2 minutes, then transfer to a bowl of cold water. Drain and peel away the skin from the cross. Chop the flesh so finely that it is almost a purée.

2 Put the tomato in a large bowl; stir in the remaining ingredients and season to taste. Mix well, cover and refrigerate for 2–3 hours.

3 Use 500–750 ml (2–3 cups) of chilled water to thin the soup to your taste. Serve well chilled, with small bowls of red onion, capsicum, spring onion, boiled egg, cucumber, fresh herbs and croutons (see pages 8–9) in the centre of the table. Diners can add their own choice of accompaniments to their individual bowls.

NUTRITION PER SERVE (6)
Protein 4 g; Fat 0.5 g; Carbohydrate 6.5 g; Dietary Fibre 3 g; Cholesterol 0 mg; 208 kJ (50 Cal)

WON TON SOUP

Preparation time: 45 minutes
Total cooking time: 20 minutes
Serves 4–6

4 dried Chinese mushrooms
4 spring onions (scallions), very finely sliced, to garnish
125 g (4½ oz) minced (ground) pork and veal
60 g (2¼ oz) raw prawn (shrimp) meat, finely chopped
3 teaspoons soy sauce
1 teaspoon sesame oil
1 spring onion (scallion), finely sliced
2 teaspoons grated ginger
1 tablespoon finely chopped water chestnuts
24 won ton wrappers
1.25 litres (5 cups) chicken stock

1 Cover the mushrooms in enough hot water and soak for 30 minutes. Meanwhile, put the very fine strips of spring onion in a bowl of icy cold water (this makes the strips curl).
2 Squeeze the mushrooms dry with your hands. Remove the stems and chop the caps finely. Mix together the mushrooms, mince, prawn meat, soy sauce, sesame oil, spring onion, ginger, water chestnuts and salt to taste.
3 Working with only one won ton wrapper at a time (cover the rest with a damp tea towel), place a teaspoon of the filling in the centre of each wrapper. Moisten the edges with a little water and bring the sides up to form a pouch. Set aside on a plate dusted with flour while making the rest.
4 Cook the won tons in batches in a large pan of rapidly boiling water for 4–5 minutes; remove and drain. Bring the stock to the boil in another pan. Put the won tons in small bowls, garnish with the curls of spring onion and pour in the hot stock.

NUTRITION PER SERVE (6)
Protein 12 g; Fat 1 g; Carbohydrate 25 g; Dietary Fibre 3 g; Cholesterol 30 mg; 650 kJ (155 Cal)

COOK'S FILE

Note: Won ton wrappers are available from Asian food stores and can be frozen very successfully.

Slice the spring onions very finely and leave in iced water to make them curl.

Gently squeeze the excess liquid from the rehydrated mushrooms.

Moisten the edges of the wrapper and bring the sides up to make a pouch.

Cook the won tons in batches in a large pan of rapidly boiling water.

JERUSALEM ARTICHOKE SOUP

Preparation time: 20 minutes
Total cooking time: 55 minutes
Serves 4

1 kg (2 lb 4 oz) Jerusalem artichokes, peeled
25 g (1 oz) butter
1 onion, finely chopped
625 ml (2½ cups) chicken stock
250 ml (1 cup) milk
170 ml (⅔ cup) cream

1 Cut any large artichokes so they are all an even size. Melt the butter in a large heavy-based pan and add the artichoke and onion. Cook over low heat, covered, for 10 minutes, stirring occasionally: they should not brown.

2 Add the stock and milk and bring to the boil. Reduce the heat, cover and simmer for 40 minutes, or until the vegetables are very soft.

3 Cool, then purée in batches until very smooth. Return to the pan, reheat gently, season and add the cream.

NUTRITION PER SERVE
Protein 7 g; Fat 23 g; Carbohydrate 10 g; Dietary Fibre 9 g; Cholesterol 75 mg; 1182 kJ (280 Cal)

COOK'S FILE

Note: Jerusalem artichoke is related to the sunflower rather than the globe artichoke. 'Jerusalem' is derived from *girasole*, Italian for sunflower.

Scrub the artichokes well and peel with a potato peeler.

Cut the artichokes so that they are all an even size.

Leave the soup to simmer for 40 minutes until the vegetables are soft.

SPICY RED LENTIL SOUP

Preparation time: 15 minutes
Total cooking time: 35 minutes
Serves 4–6

2 tablespoons oil
1 medium onion, finely chopped
1 teaspoon ground cumin
1 teaspoon ground coriander
1/4 teaspoon ground allspice
2 garlic cloves, crushed
500 g (1 lb 2 oz) red lentils
1.25–1.5 litres (5–6 cups) vegetable stock
90 g (1/3 cup) thick plain yoghurt

1 Heat the oil in a heavy-based pan. Cook the onion over medium heat for 5 minutes, until soft. Stir in the spices and garlic for 1 minute.
2 Add the lentils, stirring to coat well with spices. Pour in the stock and stir well. Bring to the boil, then reduce the heat and simmer, partially covered with a loose-fitting lid, for 30 minutes.
3 Add a little more vegetable stock if you prefer a thinner soup and serve with a dollop of yoghurt on top.

NUTRITION PER SERVE (6)
Protein 20 g; Fat 9 g; Carbohydrate 30 g; Dietary Fibre 12 g; Cholesterol 2 mg; 1219 kJ (290 Cal)

COOK'S FILE

Storage time: This soup will keep for 1 day in the fridge, but becomes quite thick on standing—thin it down with stock or water.
Note: Red lentils do not need soaking prior to cooking.

An easy way to crush garlic is to bruise and scrape it with the side of a knife.

Add the spices and garlic to the softened onion and cook for 1 minute further.

Add the lentils to the pan and stir them well to coat with spices.

TOM KHA GAI
(Thai Chicken and Coconut Milk Soup)

Preparation time: 20 minutes
Total cooking time: 10 minutes
Serves 4

625 ml (2 1/2 cups) chicken stock
2 makrut (kaffir) lime leaves
5 cm (2 inch) piece lemon grass, white part only, finely chopped
3 cm (1 1/4 inch) piece galangal, cut into 4 pieces lengthways
2 tablespoons fish sauce
2 tablespoons lime juice
1 chicken breast fillet, finely sliced
120 g (4 1/4 oz) drained canned straw mushrooms
375 ml (1 1/2 cups) coconut milk
3–4 teaspoons palm sugar
2 small red chillies, split
hot chilli sauce, to serve

1 Heat the stock in a medium pan, add the lime leaves, lemon grass, galangal, fish sauce and lime juice. Bring to the boil.
2 Add the chicken, mushrooms and coconut milk. Reduce the heat and simmer for 3–5 minutes, stirring all the time, until the chicken is cooked.
3 Add the sugar and chillies and cook for 1 minute. Serve garnished with hot chilli sauce.

NUTRITION PER SERVE
Protein 11 g; Fat 20 g; Carbohydrate 8 g; Dietary Fibre 3 g; Cholesterol 15 mg; 1065 kJ (254 Cal)

COOK'S FILE

Hint: When working with chillies avoid smarting by wearing a pair of disposable gloves (or wash your hands thoroughly with soapy water before touching your eyes or lips).

Lemon grass, makrut (kaffir) limes and galangal are available from Asian stores.

Add the chicken, straw mushrooms and coconut milk.

Add the palm sugar and small red chillies and cook for 1 minute further.

Spicy Red Lentil Soup (top) and Tom Kha Gai

PASTE
NET850

CHEESE SOUP

Preparation time: 20 minutes
Total cooking time: 15 minutes
Serves 4–6

75 g (2½ oz) butter
3 spring onions (scallions), finely chopped
60 g (½ cup) plain (all-purpose) flour
875 ml (3½ cups) chicken stock
250 ml (1 cup) milk
100 g (3½ oz) pumpkin, grated
150 g (5½ oz) grated Cheddar
crusty bread rolls, to serve

1 Melt the butter in a heavy-based pan and cook the spring onion for 3 minutes, until soft. Add the flour and stir for 2 minutes until smooth. Add the combined stock and milk gradually, stirring until smooth.

2 Add the pumpkin and bring to the boil, then reduce the heat and simmer for 10 minutes. Stir in the cheese until melted and smooth.

3 Cut the tops from the bread rolls and hollow out the centres. Heat in a preheated 180°C (350°F/Gas 4) oven until warm, then use as soup bowls.

NUTRITION PER SERVE (6)
Protein 11 g; Fat 20 g; Carbohydrate 20 g; Dietary Fibre 1 g; Cholesterol 63 mg; 1270 kJ (305 Cal)

Peel the pumpkin and finely grate it using the coarse side of a grater.

Add the stock and milk gradually and stir continuously to prevent lumps forming.

Add the grated cheese to the pan and stir until melted and smooth.

HOMESTYLE VEGETABLE SOUP

Preparation time: 25 minutes + overnight soaking
Total cooking time: 55 minutes
Serves 6

220 g (8 oz) dried soup mix
2 tablespoons oil
1 large onion, finely chopped
1 green capsicum (pepper), chopped
2 zucchini (courgettes), sliced
2 sticks celery, sliced
125 g ($4^1/2$ oz) button mushrooms, sliced
2 carrots, sliced
1 large potato, chopped
500 g (1 lb 2 oz) pumpkin, peeled, chopped
2 litres (8 cups) vegetable stock

1 Soak the soup mix in water for 8 hours, then drain. Heat the oil in a large heavy-based pan and cook the onion for 5 minutes, until soft. Add the capsicum, zucchini, celery and mushrooms and cook for 5 minutes.

2 Add the sliced carrot, potato and pumpkin and stir to combine. Pour in the stock and add the soup mix; bring to the boil, then reduce the heat.

3 Partially cover the pan and simmer for 45 minutes, until the vegetables and soup mix are very soft.

NUTRITION PER SERVE
Protein 5 g; Fat 7 g; Carbohydrate 15 g; Dietary Fibre 5 g; Cholesterol 0.5 mg; 595 kJ (140 Cal)

COOK'S FILE

Storage time: Keep for 2 days in the refrigerator or freeze for 1 month.

Cover the soup mix with water and leave to soak and rehydrate.

Pour the stock into the pan over the chopped vegetables.

Partially cover the pan and simmer until the vegetables are very soft.

GARLIC SOUP

Preparation time: 20 minutes
Total cooking time: 25 minutes
Serves 4

1 bulb garlic (about 20 cloves)
2 large sprigs thyme
1 litre (4 cups) chicken stock
80 ml (1/3 cup) cream
4 thick slices white bread
fresh thyme, to garnish

1 Crush each clove of garlic with the side of a knife. Discard the skin and place the garlic in a large pan with the thyme, stock and 250 ml (1 cup) water. Bring to the boil, then reduce the heat and simmer gently for 20 minutes.

2 Strain the soup through a fine sieve into a clean pan. Add the cream and reheat gently, without allowing to boil. Season to taste.

3 Trim and discard the crusts from the bread and cut the bread into cubes about 3 cm (1 1/4 inch) square. Spread these out on a flat oven tray and cook in a preheated 180°C (350°F/Gas 4) oven for 5–10 minutes, until lightly golden. Put the bread into four serving bowls and pour the soup over the bread. Garnish with extra thyme and serve immediately.

NUTRITION PER SERVE
Protein 4 g; Fat 10 g; Carbohydrate 15 g; Dietary Fibre 3 g; Cholesterol 28 mg; 705 kJ (170 Cal)

COOK'S FILE

Storage time: Best served same day. The bread cubes may be cooked up to 4 hours in advance and kept in an airtight container until required.
Note: The after-effects of the garlic are minimal as it has been boiled.

Bruise the cloves of garlic with the side of a knife and then discard the skin.

Strain the soup through a fine sieve into a clean pan.

Bake the bread in the oven until toasted and lightly golden.

AUTUMN GARDEN SOUP

Preparation time: 35 minutes
Total cooking time: 55 minutes
Serves 6

30 g (1 oz) butter
1 large leek, sliced
1 garlic clove, crushed
1 teaspoon grated ginger
2 parsnips, peeled and chopped
1 medium celeriac, peeled and chopped
2 large carrots, chopped
3 potatoes, chopped
2 turnips, peeled and chopped
1.125 litres (4 1/2 cups) vegetable stock
2 tablespoons chopped chives

1 Melt the butter in a large heavy-based pan and add the leek. Cook over low heat for 15 minutes until very soft and lightly golden.

2 Add the garlic and ginger and cook, stirring, for 1 minute further. Add the vegetables and stock to the pan and bring to the boil.

3 Reduce heat to simmer, partially covered, for about 40 minutes until very soft. Stir in the chives and serve.

NUTRITION PER SERVE
Protein 4 g; Fat 5 g; Carbohydrate 18 g; Dietary Fibre 6 g; Cholesterol 13 mg; 535 kJ (128 Cal)

COOK'S FILE

Storage time: The soup will keep for up to 2 days in the refrigerator.

Hint: The soup becomes very thick on standing—thin with stock or water.

Peel away the outer rough surface of the celeriac with a potato peeler.

Cook the leek until soft and golden and then add the garlic and ginger.

Simmer for about 40 minutes, until the vegetables are very soft.

ZUCCHINI SOUP

Preparation time: 15 minutes
Total cooking time: 30 minutes
Serves 4

40 g (1 1/2 oz) butter
1 onion, chopped
4 zucchini (courgettes), sliced
1 tablespoon plain (all-purpose) flour
500 ml (2 cups) chicken stock
500 ml (2 cups) milk
1 teaspoon chopped fresh thyme
125 ml (1/2 cup) cream
35 g (1/3 cup) finely grated Parmesan cheese

1 Melt the butter in a large pan and cook the onion, covered, over low heat for 5 minutes, until soft but not browned. Add the zucchini and cook, covered, for a further 5 minutes.
2 Add the flour to the pan and stir over low heat for 1 minute. Gradually add the stock and milk, stirring after each addition. Add the thyme and increase the heat to bring to the boil.
3 Reduce the heat and simmer for 15 minutes. Cool, then purée in batches until smooth. Reheat gently and add the cream and Parmesan. Stir until the cheese has melted, but do not allow the soup to boil. Season to taste before serving.

NUTRITION PER SERVE
Protein 15 g; Fat 35 g; Carbohydrate 12 g; Dietary Fibre 2 g; Cholesterol 105 mg; 1690 kJ (405 Cal)

COOK'S FILE

Storage time: Refrigerate for 1 day without the cream and cheese—add these when you reheat.

Add the stock and milk gradually, stirring after each addition.

Add the chopped fresh thyme and return to the heat.

Do not allow the soup to boil again once you have added the cream and cheese.

Add the spices to the pan with the onion and stir to thoroughly combine.

Add the stock to the mixture of spices and vegetables.

Saffron threads are expensive but will add a subtle flavour and golden colour.

Do not stir in the couscous until you are ready to serve the soup.

CHICKEN AND COUSCOUS SOUP

Preparation time: 25 minutes
Total cooking time: 30 minutes
Serves 6

1 tablespoon olive oil
1 onion, sliced
1/2 teaspoon ground cumin
1/2 teaspoon paprika
1 teaspoon grated ginger
1 garlic clove, crushed
2 sticks celery, sliced
2 small carrots, sliced
2 zucchini (courgettes), sliced
1.125 litres (4 1/2 cups) chicken stock
2 chicken breast fillets, sliced
pinch of saffron threads, optional
95 g (1/2 cup) instant couscous
2 tablespoons chopped parsley

1 Heat the oil in a large pan. Add the onion and cook over medium heat for 10 minutes until very soft, stirring occasionally. Add the spices, ginger and garlic and stir for 1 minute.
2 Add the celery, carrot and zucchini and stir to coat with spices. Stir in the stock. Bring to the boil, reduce to a simmer, partially covered, for about 15 minutes, until vegetables are tender.
3 Add the chicken and saffron threads to the pan and cook for about 5 minutes, until the chicken is just tender; do not overcook. Stir in the couscous and parsley and serve.

NUTRITION PER SERVE
Protein 24 g; Fat 6 g; Carbohydrate 53 g; Dietary Fibre 5 g; Cholesterol 37 mg; 1482 kJ (350 Cal)

COOK'S FILE

Hint: Add the couscous to the soup just before serving: it absorbs liquid quickly and becomes very thick.

CARIBBEAN BLACK BEAN SOUP

Preparation time: 20 minutes + overnight soaking
Total cooking time: 1 hour 30 minutes
Serves 6

440 g (15½ oz) dried black beans
2 tablespoons oil
1 large onion, sliced
1 teaspoon ground coriander
2 teaspoons ground cumin
½ teaspoon chilli powder
2 garlic cloves, crushed
300 g (10½ oz) bacon bones
2 tablespoons red wine vinegar
1 tablespoon soft brown sugar
3 spring onions (scallions), finely chopped
1 tablespoon chopped parsley
2 hard-boiled eggs, chopped

1 Put the beans in a large bowl, cover with water and soak overnight. Drain.
2 Heat the oil in a large pan, cook the onion over medium heat for 5 minutes, until softened. Add the coriander, cumin, chilli powder and garlic to the pan and cook for 1 minute.
3 Add the bacon bones and 1.125 litres (4½ cups) water, stirring well to scrape the spices from the base of the pan. Add the beans and bring to the boil, then reduce the heat to simmer, partially covered, for 1–1½ hours, until the beans are very soft.
4 Use a pair of tongs or forks to remove the bacon bones from the pan and discard. Stir in the vinegar and sugar. Season. For a thicker soup, mash the beans slightly with a potato masher. Garnish with spring onions, parsley and hard-boiled egg to serve.

NUTRITION PER SERVE
Protein 24 g; Fat 22 g; Carbohydrate 10 g; Dietary Fibre 15 g; Cholesterol 70 mg; 1377 kJ (330 Cal)

COOK'S FILE

Note: Black beans are also known as turtle beans and are available at good delicatessens. They are not to be confused with Chinese black beans.
Storage time: Keeps, covered and refrigerated, for up to 2 days, but will become very thick. Thin down with chicken stock or water to reheat.

Add the cumin, coriander, chilli powder and garlic to the softened onion.

Add the bacon bones to the spices and onion in the pan.

Add the black beans to the pan and bring to the boil.

Use a pair of tongs to lift the bacon bones from the pan and discard.

CORN CHOWDER

Preparation time: 10 minutes
Total cooking time: 30 minutes
Serves 6

60 g (2¼ oz) butter
1 large onion, finely chopped
1 garlic clove, crushed
2 potatoes, cubed
1 litre (4 cups) chicken stock
420 g (15 oz) can creamed corn
420 g (15 oz) can corn kernels, drained
pinch cayenne pepper, optional
60 ml (¼ cup) cream
2 tablespoons chopped chives

1 Heat the butter in a large heavy-based pan and cook the onion, stirring, for 5 minutes, or until soft and lightly golden. Add the garlic and cook for a further minute.

2 Add the potato and stock and bring to the boil. Reduce the heat and leave to simmer for 10 minutes, add the cans of creamed corn and drained corn kernels and simmer for a further 10 minutes.

3 Season with salt, pepper and cayenne pepper to taste and stir in the cream and chives. Reheat gently, without allowing the soup to come to the boil, and serve immediately.

NUTRITION PER SERVE
Protein 5 g; Fat 15 g; Carbohydrate 32 g; Dietary Fibre 6 g; Cholesterol 40 mg; 1140 kJ (275 Cal)

Stir-fry the onion in butter until it is soft and golden.

Add the cans of creamed corn and corn kernels to the simmering soup.

Stir in the cream and chives at the end of cooking time.

SEAFOOD LAKSA

Preparation time: 45 minutes
Total cooking time: 40–45 minutes
Serves 4–6

1 kg (2 lb 4 oz) medium raw prawns (shrimp)
125 ml (1/2 cup) oil
2–6 large red chillies, seeded
1 large onion, roughly chopped
3 garlic cloves, peeled
2 cm (3/4 inch) piece ginger or galangal
1 teaspoon turmeric
1 tablespoon ground coriander
3 x 6 cm (2 1/2 inch) stalks lemon grass, white part only
1–2 teaspoons shrimp paste
600 ml (21 fl oz) coconut cream
4 makrut (kaffir) lime leaves
2 teaspoons salt
2 teaspoons palm sugar
200 g (7 oz) packet fish balls
190 g (6 3/4 oz) packet fried bean curd pieces
250 g (9 oz) thin fresh egg noodles
250 g (9 oz) fresh bean sprouts
20 g (1/3 cup) chopped fresh mint, to serve
15 g (1/4 cup) coriander (cilantro) leaves, to serve

1 Peel and devein the prawns (use a toothpick or large needle to remove the vein without having to cut the prawn). Leave the tails intact and reserve the heads and shells.

2 Heat 2 tablespoons of the oil in a large pan, add the prawn heads and shells and stir-fry until the heads are bright orange. Add 1 litre (4 cups) water, bring to the boil, then reduce the heat and simmer for 15 minutes. Strain the stock, discarding the shells.

3 Place the chillies, onion, garlic, ginger, turmeric, coriander, lemon grass and 60 ml (1/4 cup) of the prawn stock in a food processor and process until almost smooth.

4 Heat the remaining oil in the clean pan, add the processed mixture and shrimp paste. Stir over low heat for 3 minutes, until fragrant. Add the prawn stock and leave to simmer for 10 minutes. Add the coconut cream, lime leaves, salt and sugar and allow to simmer, uncovered, for a further 5 minutes.

5 Add the prawns to the pan and simmer for 2 minutes until they are just pink. Lift the prawns out of the laksa with a slotted spoon and set aside. Add the fish balls and bean curd and simmer gently.

6 Bring a pan of water to the boil, add the noodles, cook for 2 minutes and drain. Remove the tails from the bean sprouts. Put the noodles in a large tureen or individual bowls and top with bean sprouts and prawns. Ladle the hot soup into the bowls and sprinkle with mint and coriander leaves to serve. For a really fiery soup, garnish with extra sliced red chilli.

NUTRITION PER SERVE
Protein 50 g; Fat 45 g; Carbohydrate 40 g; Dietary Fibre 7 g; Cholesterol 280 mg; 3215 kJ (770 Cal)

COOK'S FILE

Note: Laksa originated in Singapore and can also be made using fresh or dried rice noodles. Shredded cucumber can be added with the bean sprouts.
Variation: Laksa can be made without the fish balls and bean curd. Instead, use a combination of seafood or replace the seafood with bite-sized pieces of chicken or pork.

Chopping chillies can lead to smarting eyes and skin so wear gloves.

Peel and devein the prawns, leaving the tails intact and reserving the heads.

Stir-fry the prawn heads and shells until they are bright orange.

Process the onion, garlic and spices with a little prawn stock until almost smooth.

Add the prawns and cook for 2 minutes until they are just pink.

Add the fish balls. Cut the bean curd into triangles for a traditional laksa.

GOULASH SOUP

Preparation time: 15 minutes
Total cooking time: 1 hour 15 minutes
Serves 4–6

650 g (1 lb 7 oz) blade steak
2 tablespoons oil
1 large leek, sliced
2 garlic cloves, crushed
1 teaspoon paprika
1 teaspoon caraway seeds
400 g (14 oz) can crushed tomatoes
1 litre (4 cups) beef stock
2 potatoes, diced
sour cream, to serve

1 Cut the meat into small cubes. Heat the oil in a large pan, brown the meat in batches and set aside.

2 Add the leek to the pan and cook for 5 minutes until soft. Add the garlic and paprika and cook for 1 minute. Add the seeds, tomatoes, stock and meat. Bring to the boil, then simmer, partially covered, for 30 minutes.

3 Add the potatoes and simmer for 30 minutes, until very tender. Serve with sour cream.

NUTRITION PER SERVE (6)
Protein 25 g; Fat 17 g; Carbohydrate 9 g; Dietary Fibre 2 g; Cholesterol 75 mg; 1220 kJ (290 Cal)

COOK'S FILE

Storage time: The soup will keep for up to 2 days in the refrigerator.

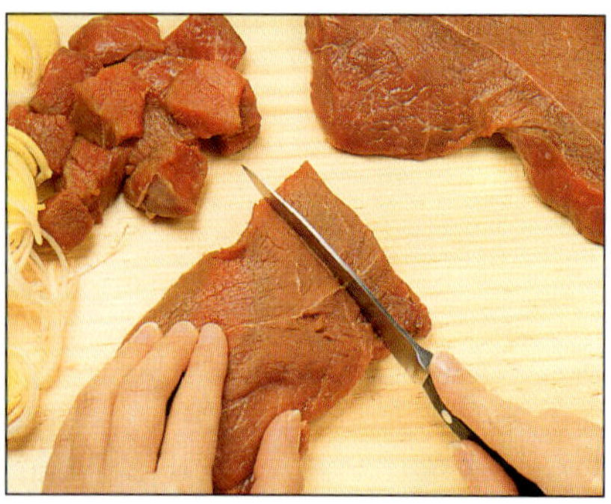

Trim the blade steak of any fat and sinew when you cut it into small cubes.

Brown the meat in small batches so that it fries rather than stews.

Add the caraway seeds, tomatoes, stock and meat to the pan.

AVGOLEMONO

(Greek Egg and Lemon Soup)

Preparation time: 20 minutes
Total cooking time: 10 minutes
Serves 4–6

1.5 litres (6 cups) chicken stock
150 g (3/4 cup) long-grain rice
2 eggs, separated
125 ml (1/2 cup) lemon juice

1 Bring the stock to the boil in a large heavy-based pan. Add the rice and allow to simmer for 8–10 minutes until tender.
2 Beat the egg whites in a large dry mixing bowl until soft peaks form. Add the yolks and beat until they are combined.
3 Gradually pour in the lemon juice and then about 1–2 cups of the rice and stock soup, beating continuously. Gradually fold this into the pan of rice soup and serve immediately.

NUTRITION PER SERVE (6)
Protein 4 g; Fat 2 g; Carbohydrate 20 g; Dietary Fibre 0.5 g; Cholesterol 60 mg; 500 kJ (120 Cal)

COOK'S FILE

Hint: Assemble all the ingredients and utensils beforehand, work quickly and serve this soup immediately—it does not reheat well.
Variation: Egg and lemon soup can also be made with fish stock instead of the chicken stock.

Beat the egg whites in a large dry mixing bowl until soft peaks form.

Beat continuously while you pour in the lemon juice and stock.

To keep the soup light and fluffy, use a large metal spoon to fold gently.

ASPARAGUS SOUP WITH PARMESAN CRISPS

Preparation time: 5 minutes
Total cooking time: 35 minutes
Serves 4

60 g (2 1/4 oz) butter
750 g (1 lb 10 oz) fresh asparagus spears, finely chopped
1 small onion, chopped
30 g (1/4 cup) plain (all-purpose) flour
750 ml (3 cups) chicken stock
125 ml (1/2 cup) cream
100 g (3 1/2 oz) fresh Parmesan cheese

1 Heat the butter in a large heavy-based pan and cook the asparagus and onion, stirring, over medium heat for about 5 minutes, until the onion is soft. Sprinkle with the flour and stir for 1 minute to combine.
2 Remove from the heat and add the stock gradually, stirring until smooth. Return to the heat, bring to the boil, then reduce the heat and simmer, covered, for about 20 minutes, until the asparagus is tender.
3 Allow to cool a little for easier and safer handling, before processing in batches until smooth. Return to the pan, stir in the cream and then reheat gently without allowing the soup to boil. Season to taste and serve straight away with Parmesan Crisps.
4 To make the Parmesan Crisps, finely grate the cheese. Heat a non-stick frying pan until moderately hot. Sprinkle 25 g (1/4 cup) of the cheese into a 10 cm (4 inch) round in the pan. Cook until melted and bubbling, then remove the pan from the heat. When the bubbling subsides and the cheese hardens slightly, lift the crisp out with a spatula onto a paper towel. Repeat to make 4 large crisps.

NUTRITION PER SERVE
Protein 18 g; Fat 35 g; Carbohydrate 20 g; Dietary Fibre 4 g; Cholesterol 105 mg; 1910 kJ (455 Cal)

COOK'S FILE

Note: If possible, buy a chunk of Parmigiano Reggiano from a good delicatessen—this is the best Parmesan.

Choose tender young asparagus spears and chop them finely.

Cook the asparagus and onion, stirring over medium heat until the onion is soft.

Once the soup has been processed, stir in the cream.

Use a spatula to lift the Parmesan Crisps out of the pan onto paper towels.

CURRIED SWEET POTATO SOUP

Preparation time: 20 minutes
Total cooking time: 40 minutes
Serves 6

1 tablespoon oil
1 large onion, chopped
2 garlic cloves, crushed
3 teaspoons curry powder
1.25 kg (2 lb 12 oz) orange sweet potato, peeled and cubed
1 litre (4 cups) chicken stock
1 large apple, peeled, cored and grated
125 ml (1/2 cup) coconut cream

1 Heat the oil in a large pan and cook the onion over medium heat for 10 minutes, stirring occasionally, until very soft. Add the garlic and curry powder and cook for a minute further.

2 Add the sweet potato, stock and apple and stir to combine. Bring to the boil, reduce the heat and simmer, partially covered, for 30 minutes, until the sweet potato is very soft.

3 Allow the soup to cool a little before processing in batches until smooth. Return to the pan, stir in the coconut cream and reheat gently without boiling. Delicious served with warmed pitta bread.

NUTRITION PER SERVE
Protein 5 g; Fat 8 g; Carbohydrate 35 g; Dietary Fibre 5.5 g; Cholesterol 0 mg; 975 kJ (233 Cal)

COOK'S FILE

Storage time: Can be kept in the fridge for 1 day without the coconut cream: add this before reheating.

Add the garlic and curry powder to the softened onion.

Stir in the stock with the cubed sweet potato and grated apple.

Once the soup has been processed stir in the coconut cream.

SPINACH AND POTATO SOUP

Preparation time: 20 minutes
Total cooking time: 45 minutes
Serves 6

30 g (1 oz) butter
1 large leek, sliced
2 garlic cloves, crushed
1 bunch English spinach
4 potatoes, chopped
1 litre (4 cups) vegetable stock
125 ml (1/2 cup) sour cream

1 Melt the butter in a large heavy-based pan. Add the leek and cook over medium heat for 10 minutes, stirring occasionally, until very soft. Add the crushed garlic and cook for a further minute.

2 Wash the spinach very thoroughly to avoid any grittiness; discard the stalks and shred the leaves. Add to the pan with the potato and stock and bring to the boil. Reduce the heat and leave to simmer, partially covered, for about 30 minutes, until the potatoes are very soft.

3 Allow to cool a little for ease of handling, before processing in batches until smooth. Return to the pan and reheat gently without allowing to boil. Stir in the sour cream and add salt and pepper to taste.

NUTRITION PER SERVE
Protein 4 g; Fat 13 g; Carbohydrate 15 g; Dietary Fibre 2.5 g; Cholesterol 40 mg; 780 kJ (185 Cal)

COOK'S FILE

Storage time: If necessary, soup can be refrigerated for 1 day.
Note: If you can't find English spinach, use silverbeet (Swiss chard).

Cook the leek over medium heat until it is very soft.

Discard the stalks of the spinach and chop the leaves into shreds.

Partially cover with a loose-fitting lid and simmer until the potatoes are soft.

CREAM OF CAULIFLOWER SOUP

Preparation time: 20 minutes
Total cooking time: 15–20 minutes
Serves 4–6

750 g (1 lb 10 oz) cauliflower
1 tablespoon oil
750 ml (3 cups) chicken stock
250 ml (1 cup) cream
1/4 teaspoon ground nutmeg
salt and ground black pepper, to taste

1 Cut the cauliflower into small even-sized florets. Heat the oil in a large heavy-based pan and stir-fry the cauliflower for 3 minutes, or until it is just starting to soften.

2 Add the stock to the pan, cover and simmer for 10–15 minutes until the cauliflower is tender.

3 Stir in the cream and set the soup aside to cool a little. Use a food processor or blender to process in batches until smooth. Return to the pan and add the nutmeg, salt and pepper to taste. Heat through gently and serve immediately.

NUTRITION PER SERVE (6)
Protein 4 g; Fat 21 g; Carbohydrate 4 g; Dietary Fibre 2 g; Cholesterol 55 mg; 915 kJ (220 Cal)

COOK'S FILE

Note: Even those who dislike cauliflower will usually enjoy this delicately flavoured soup. Choose very fresh cauliflower with a firm head and no brown or black spots.
Variation: For an even richer soup, add 125 g (1 cup) grated Cheddar with the nutmeg and seasonings. Garnish with tiny steamed cauliflower florets, or a sprig of fresh chervil.

Use a sharp knife to cut the cauliflower into small, even-sized florets.

Stir-fry the cauliflower for 3 minutes until it is starting to soften.

Once the cauliflower is tender, stir in the cream and then process.

Spinach and Potato Soup (top) and Cream of Cauliflower Soup

RATATOUILLE AND PASTA SOUP

Preparation time: 25 minutes
Total cooking time: 40 minutes
Serves 6

1 medium eggplant (aubergine), chopped
1 tablespoon olive oil
1 large onion, chopped
1 large red and 1 large green capsicum (pepper), chopped
2 garlic cloves, crushed
3 zucchini (courgettes), sliced
2 x 400 g (14 oz) cans crushed tomatoes
1 teaspoon dried oregano leaves
$1/2$ teaspoon dried thyme leaves
1 litre (4 cups) vegetable stock
80 g ($2\frac{3}{4}$ oz) pasta spirals

1 Place the eggplant in a colander and sprinkle generously with salt. Leave for 20 minutes; rinse and pat dry with paper towels.

2 Heat the oil in a large pan and cook the onion for 10 minutes, until soft and lightly golden. Add the capsicum, garlic, zucchini and eggplant and cook for 5 minutes.

3 Add the tomatoes, herbs and stock. Bring to the boil, reduce the heat and simmer for 10 minutes, until tender. Add the pasta and cook for 15 minutes, until tender. Serve with Parmesan.

NUTRITION PER SERVE
Protein 6 g; Fat 4 g; Carbohydrate 23 g; Dietary Fibre 5 g; Cholesterol 0 mg; 635 kJ (150 Cal)

COOK'S FILE

Storage time: Soup will keep for up to 2 days in the refrigerator.

Put the chopped eggplant in a colander and sprinkle generously with salt.

Add the capsicum, garlic, zucchini and eggplant to the pan.

Once the vegetables are tender, add the pasta to the pan.

Use a sharp knife to chop the two bulbs of fennel.

Remove the oysters from the shells with a small spoon, avoiding any grit.

The oysters are cooked when they just begin to curl at the edges.

Spread the pitta breads with butter and sprinkle with sesame seeds.

FENNEL AND OYSTER SOUP WITH SESAME PITTAS

Preparation time: 25 minutes
Total cooking time: 40 minutes
Serves 4–6

40 g (1 1/2 oz) butter
1 medium onion, chopped
2 fennel bulbs (600 g/1 lb 5 oz), chopped
500 ml (2 cups) fish stock
125 ml (1/2 cup) dry white wine
125 ml (1/2 cup) cream
1/2 teaspoon nutmeg
24 oysters, opened
1 teaspoon lemon juice
salt and white pepper
2 tablespoons chopped parsley, to serve

Sesame Pittas
2 small pitta breads
60 g (2 1/4 oz) butter, melted
2 teaspoons sesame seeds

1 Melt the butter in a large heavy-based pan and cook the onion over medium heat for 5 minutes, until soft but not browned. Add the fennel and cook, covered, for 5 minutes. Add the stock, wine and 125 ml (1/2 cup) water, bring to the boil, reduce the heat to simmer, partially covered, for 30 minutes, until the fennel is very soft.

2 Allow to cool before processing in batches until smooth. Return to the pan and reheat gently. Stir in the cream, nutmeg and oysters (and any liquid in the shells).

3 Simmer until the oysters just begin to curl at the edges (about 2 minutes). Do not overcook or the oysters will be tough. Stir in the lemon juice and add salt and pepper to taste. Garnish with chopped parsley.

4 To make Sesame Pittas: preheat the oven to 200°C (400°F/Gas 6). Split the breads in half and brush both sides with melted butter; put them on a baking tray and sprinkle with sesame seeds. Bake for about 10 minutes, or until golden and crisp, and serve immediately.

NUTRITION PER SERVE (6)
Protein 7 g; Fat 25 g; Carbohydrate 18 g; Dietary Fibre 4 g; Cholesterol 85 mg; 1325 kJ (317 Cal)

JUNGLE SOUP

Preparation time: 10 minutes
Total cooking time: 35 minutes
Serves 4

2 teaspoons oil
1 medium onion, finely sliced
225 g (8 oz) butternut pumpkin, peeled and diced
225 g (8 oz) fresh pineapple or mango, chopped
1 garlic clove, crushed
1 dried red chilli, finely chopped
2 teaspoons grated ginger
1 litre (4 cups) chicken stock
2 tablespoons lime juice
350 g (12 oz) chicken breast, skinned, cut diagonally into thin strips

1 Heat the oil in a large heavy-based pan and cook the onion for 5 minutes, or until golden. Add the pumpkin and cook for 5 minutes, or until just brown. Add the pineapple, garlic, chilli and ginger and toss together.

2 Add the stock and lime juice, bring to the boil and then reduce the heat to simmer for 20 minutes, or until the pumpkin is nearly tender.

3 Add the chicken and simmer for 5 minutes, or until the chicken is cooked. Serve immediately.

NUTRITION PER SERVE
Protein 22 g; Fat 4 g; Carbohydrate 10 g; Dietary Fibre 2.5 g; Cholesterol 45 mg; 700 kJ (170 Cal)

Peel and chop the pineapple or mango into bite-sized pieces.

Add the pumpkin to the onion in the pan and cook until browned.

Use two wooden spoons to toss together the contents of the pan.

MEXICAN CORN SOUP

Preparation time: 20 minutes
Total cooking time: 30 minutes
Serves 4–6

800 g (4 cups) fresh corn kernels, off the cob
1.125 litres (4 1/2 cups) vegetable stock
30 g (1 oz) butter
1 teaspoon paprika
30 g (1/2 cup) chopped spring onions (scallions)
1/2–1 teaspoon Tabasco
125 g (1/2 cup) sour cream
2 green chillies, chopped

1 Put 600 g (3 cups) of the corn and the stock in a blender or food processor. Process for 30 seconds until smooth.
2 Heat the butter in a large pan, stir in the paprika and spring onion over medium heat for 2 minutes, or until soft.
3 Add the corn purée to the pan and bring to the boil. Reduce the heat to low and simmer for 10 minutes. Add the remaining cup of whole corn kernels and return to the boil. Reduce the heat to low and leave to simmer, for 15 minutes, or until the soup is thick. Stir in the Tabasco sauce and serve topped with a dollop or sour cream and the chopped chillies.

NUTRITION PER SERVE (6)
Protein 5 g; Fat 14 g; Carbohydrate 25 g; Dietary Fibre 4 g; Cholesterol 40 mg; 995 kJ (238 Cal)

Use a food processor to purée the corn and stock until smooth.

Stir-fry the spring onions in the butter and paprika until soft.

Add the remaining cup of whole corn kernels to give texture to the soup.

Breads and Dampers

Nothing transforms a humble bowl of soup or stew into a complete meal as successfully, or tastily, as a hunk of warm, freshly baked bread. The wonderful advantage to damper is that it can be cooked up quickly from a few store-cupboard standbys. Originally a staple food for early European settlers in outback Australia, it was a simple dough of flour and water cooked directly in the hot ashes of an open fire. These days the term refers to round leavened bread with a crunchy crust and a taste and texture similar to that of fresh white bread. The name comes from a British dialect word meaning 'something that takes the edge off the appetite'. The following recipes all serve 4 people.

HERB DAMPER

Sift 375 g (3 cups) of self-raising flour and 1 teaspoon salt into a large bowl. Stir in 30 g (1/2 cup) of chopped fresh herbs of your choice: try chives, parsley, oregano or coriander (cilantro). Make a well in the centre; combine 90 g (3 1/4 oz) melted butter, 125 ml (1/2 cup) of water and 125 ml (1/2 cup) of milk and pour onto the dry ingredients. Stir with a knife until just combined and turn onto a lightly floured surface; knead briefly until just smooth. Shape the dough into a ball, put it on a greased oven tray and press into a 20 cm (8 inch) round. Using a sharp-pointed knife, score into 8 sections, without cutting all the way through. Brush with a little extra milk and dust lightly with extra flour. Bake in a preheated 210°C (415°C/Gas 6–7) oven for 10 minutes, then reduce the heat to 180°C (350°F/Gas 4) and bake for a further 15 minutes, or until the damper is golden and sounds hollow when tapped.

Clockwise from top left: Herb Damper; Pumpkin Rounds; Onion Bread; Cheese, Olive and Rosemary Dampers

CHEESE, OLIVE AND ROSEMARY DAMPERS

Sift 250 g (2 cups) of self-raising flour and 1 teaspoon salt into a large mixing bowl. Add 30 g (1 oz) chopped butter and use your fingertips to rub the butter into the flour until it resembles fine breadcrumbs. Stir in 50 g (½ cup) of freshly grated Parmesan cheese, 60 g (½ cup) of sliced black pitted olives and 1 tablespoon chopped fresh rosemary. Make a well in the centre and pour in the combined 125 ml (½ cup) milk and 60 ml (¼ cup) buttermilk. Mix to form a soft dough using a knife. Turn the dough onto a lightly floured surface and knead briefly until just smooth. Divide the dough into 4 equal portions and shape each into a round ball and flatten out to a 2 cm (¾ inch) thick round. Place on a greased oven tray, leaving room to expand. Brush with a little extra milk and score a cross on the top of each. Sprinkle with a little extra grated Parmesan and bake in a preheated oven 210°C (415°C/Gas 6–7), for 20 minutes, or until golden brown and crusty.
Variation: Try other chopped herbs such as oregano, parsley or chives in place of rosemary.

PUMPKIN ROUNDS

Sift 310 g (2½ cups) of self-raising flour and ½ teaspoon ground nutmeg into a bowl. Add 60 g (2¼ oz) chopped butter and use your fingertips to rub the butter into the flour until it resembles fine breadcrumbs. Make a well in the centre. Mix together 1 egg, 250 g (1 cup) of cooked mashed pumpkin (350 g/12 oz raw) and 1-2 tablespoons milk and pour onto the dry ingredients. Stir with a knife until just combined, then turn onto a lightly floured surface and knead gently until just smooth. Press the mixture out gently until about 2 cm (¾ inch) thick, then cut into 7 cm (2¾ inch) rounds. Place closely together on a greased oven tray and brush with a little extra milk. Bake in a preheated 210°C (415°C/Gas 6–7) oven for 15-20 minutes, or until the tops are lightly golden. Serve warm or cold with soup or stew.
Variations: Add 40 g (⅓ cup) of grated Cheddar cheese to the combined egg and pumpkin mixture or 4 tablespoons of chopped fresh herbs of your choice.

ONION BREAD

Heat a little olive oil in a frying pan, add a large, finely chopped onion and cook over medium heat until golden. Sift 375 g (3 cups) of self-raising flour into a large mixing bowl and stir in a 35 g (1¼ oz) sachet French onion or tomato soup mix and the cooked onion. Make a well in the centre and stir in 500 ml (2 cups) of buttermilk to form a soft sticky dough. Turn onto a well-floured surface, taking care to flour your hands and the surface of the dough. Gently and quickly mix in enough extra flour to form a smooth ball. Place the dough on a greased baking tray and shape into a long loaf. Score a criss-cross pattern on top, brush the top with milk and sprinkle with a little rock or sea salt. Bake in a preheated 180°C (350°F/Gas 4) oven for 50-60 minutes, or until the bread is browned and sounds hollow when tapped on the base. Serve warm or cold.

Accompaniments for Stews

Some stews, such as Lancashire Hotpot and Irish Stew, contain potatoes and are a complete meal in themselves, but most are best served with an accompaniment to 'sop up' their delicious sauce. 'Soppers' should not be bland, but should not rival the stew in richness and tastiness. Mashed and baked potatoes remain enduringly popular for family meals on wintry evenings, but we also have a few ideas for more interesting and exciting accompaniments. Lighter and often flavoured with herbs or spices, these are ideal for serving to guests or to accompany the more cosmopolitan stews. All of the following recipes serve 4 people.

PASTA WITH SEEDS

Cook 500 g (1 lb 2 oz) pasta in a large pan of rapidly boiling water until just tender. Drain, then return to the pan and toss through a little olive oil and 2–3 tablespoons sesame seeds. Season to taste with a little salt and pepper and serve immediately, perhaps tossed through with some chopped fresh herbs.

COUSCOUS

Place 185 g (1 cup) of instant couscous in a large heatproof bowl and add 185 ml (3/4 cup) of boiling water. Leave to stand for 3–5 minutes. Stir through 30 g (1 oz) butter with a fork, until the butter has melted and the grains have been fluffed up. Serve to accompany your favourite stew. As a variation, try stirring through 1–2 tablespoons of your favourite chopped fresh herbs or a clove of crushed garlic.

MASHED POTATOES

Peel 4 medium-sized potatoes, cut into even-sized pieces and cook in a large pan of boiling salted water until very tender. Drain thoroughly, then return to the pan while still hot and mash quickly using a potato masher or fork. Add 20–30 g (1/2–1 oz) butter and 2–3 tablespoons milk or cream. Season to taste with salt and freshly ground pepper and beat until smooth and creamy. As a variation, try sprinkling with chopped fresh herbs. Do not mash potatoes in a food processor or they will become gluey.

CREAMY POLENTA

PUMPKIN AND PARSNIP PUREE

SWEET ONION RICE

PUMPKIN AND PARSNIP PUREE

Peel 500 g (1 lb 2 oz) pumpkin and 1–2 large parsnips and cut into small, even-sized pieces. Steam or microwave in a little water until just tender, drain then mash with a fork or potato masher. Add 1/4 teaspoon ground nutmeg, 20 g (1/2 oz) butter and salt and pepper to taste and beat until smooth. Stir in 1 tablespoon chopped fresh chives. As an alternative, omit the nutmeg and chives and instead add 1–2 teaspoons ground cumin and 1–2 teaspoons soft brown sugar.

CREAMY POLENTA

Put 330 ml (1 1/3 cups) of chicken or vegetable stock and 250 ml (1 cup) of water in a heavy-based pan and bring to the boil. Stir in 150 g (1 cup) of polenta and stir over medium heat for 10 minutes, or until very thick. Remove from the heat and stir in 60–80 ml (1/4–1/3 cup) of cream and 30 g (1 oz) butter. Stir until smooth. Alternatively, omit the butter and stir in 60 ml (1/4 cup) of cream and 50 g (1/2 cup) of grated Parmesan cheese. Polenta is a delicious accompaniment to any stew.

SWEET ONION RICE

Heat 1 tablespoon olive or mustard seed oil in a large heavy-based pan. Add 1 large finely chopped onion and 1/2 teaspoon turmeric and stir over medium heat until the onion has softened. Stir in 55 g (1/3 cup) of sultanas, 2 cloves, 1 cinnamon stick and 200 g (1 cup) of long-grain rice. Cook for 1 minute then pour in enough water or stock to cover the rice by 2 cm (3/4 inch). Bring to the boil, then reduce the heat, cover and cook for 10-15 minutes, or until all the liquid has been absorbed. Remove from the heat and leave to stand, covered, for 3–5 minutes. Fluff with a fork before serving. For a plainer dish, omit the spices and sultanas.

STEWS

BEEF BOURGUIGNON

Preparation time: 20 minutes
+ marinating
Total cooking time: 2 hours
Serves 4

1 large onion, chopped
500 g (1 lb 2 oz) chuck steak, cubed
2 thyme sprigs, leaves only
1 tablespoon chopped fresh parsley
2 bay leaves, crumbled
500 ml (2 cups) good red wine
60 ml (1/4 cup) brandy
2 tablespoons olive oil
50 g (1 3/4 oz) butter
6 rashers bacon, chopped
12 small pickling onions, peeled
150 g (5 1/2 oz) button mushrooms
2 garlic cloves, chopped
2 tablespoons plain (all-purpose) flour
375 ml (1 1/2 cups) beef stock

1 Put the onion, steak, herbs, wine and brandy in a bowl and stir well to combine. Cover with plastic wrap and refrigerate for 3 hours. Drain the meat, reserving all the marinade. Pat the meat dry with paper towels.
2 Heat 1 tablespoon oil and half the butter in a large heavy-based pan. Cook the bacon and pickling onions, stirring regularly, over low heat until the onions are golden brown. Remove the onions and bacon from the pan with a slotted spoon and set aside on a plate or paper towels.
3 Add the mushrooms and garlic to the pan and cook, stirring, for about 2 minutes; lift them from the pan with a slotted spoon and set aside with the pickling onions. Add the remaining oil and butter to the pan and when they are hot add the meat in batches and brown well. Return all the meat to the pan, sprinkle with flour and toss until all the pieces are well coated.
4 Add the reserved marinade to the pan with the stock. Bring to the boil, stir well, cover and simmer over a very low heat for 1 hour 30 minutes, or until the meat is very tender. Put the browned pickling onions, bacon and mushrooms back into the pan, season to taste and cook, uncovered, for a further 15 minutes. Delicious with mashed potatoes.

NUTRITION PER SERVE
Protein 40 g; Fat 27 g; Carbohydrate 15 g; Dietary Fibre 3 g; Cholesterol 145 mg; 2440 kJ (585 Cal)

COOK'S FILE

Variation: Instead of using chuck steak you could use gravy beef. If you can't find small pickling onions use the bulbs of English spring onions.
Note: A poor quality wine can spoil the flavour of the whole dish.

Toss the meat in the flour until all the pieces are coated.

Add the browned onions, bacon and mushrooms once the meat is tender.

BOMBAY LAMB CURRY

Preparation time: 25 minutes
Total cooking time: 1 hour 25 minutes
Serves 4–6

1.5 kg (3 lb 5 oz) leg lamb, boned (ask your butcher to do this)
2 tablespoons ghee or oil
2 onions, finely chopped
2 garlic cloves, crushed
2 small green chillies, finely chopped
5 cm (2 inch) piece ginger, grated
1 1/2 teaspoons turmeric
2 teaspoons ground cumin
3 teaspoons ground coriander
1/2–1 teaspoon chilli powder
1–1 1/2 teaspoons salt
425 g (15 oz) can crushed tomatoes
2 tablespoons coconut cream

1 Cut the meat into cubes, removing any skin and fat. You will have about 1 kg (2 lb 4 oz) meat remaining. Heat the ghee or oil in a large heavy-based frying pan (with a lid). Add the onion and cook, stirring frequently, over medium high heat for 10 minutes until golden brown. Add the garlic, chilli and ginger and stir for 2 minutes, taking care not to burn them.

2 Mix together the spices and chilli powder in a small bowl. Stir to a smooth paste with 2 tablespoons water and add to the frying pan. Stir constantly for 2 minutes, taking care not to burn them.

3 Add the meat a handful at a time, stirring well to coat with spices—make sure all the meat is well-coated and browned.

4 Add the salt to taste and stir in the tomatoes. Bring to the boil, cover and reduce the heat to low. Simmer for 45–60 minutes, until the lamb is tender. Stir in the coconut cream 30 minutes before the end of the cooking time.

NUTRITION PER SERVE (6)
Protein 58 g; Fat 13 g; Carbohydrate5 g; Dietary Fibre 1.5 g; Cholesterol 165 mg; 1565 kJ (375 Cal)

COOK'S FILE

Storage time: Keep covered and refrigerated up to 3 days. The flavour improves after at least 1 day.

Cut the meat into bite-sized chunks, about 3 cm (1 1/4 inch) square.

Once the onion is golden brown, stir in the garlic, chilli and ginger.

Blend the ground spices to a smooth paste with a little water.

Add the meat a handful at a time to make sure it is thoroughly coated.

PERSIAN CHICKEN

Preparation time: 20 minutes
Total cooking time: 1 hour
Serves 6

1.5 kg (3lb 5 oz) small chicken thighs
60 g (1/2 cup) plain (all-purpose) flour
2 tablespoons olive oil
1 large onion, chopped
2 garlic cloves, chopped
1/2 teaspoon ground cinnamon
4 ripe tomatoes, chopped
6 fresh dates, pitted and halved
2 tablespoons currants
500 ml (2 cups) rich chicken stock
2 teaspoons finely grated lemon zest
80 g (1/2 cup) almonds, toasted and roughly chopped
2 tablespoons chopped fresh parsley

1 Coat the chicken pieces with flour and shake off any excess. Heat the oil in a large heavy-based pan over moderate heat. Brown the chicken on all sides, turning regularly, and then remove from the pan. Drain any excess oil from the pan.

2 Add the onion, garlic and ground cinnamon to the pan and cook for 5 minutes, stirring regularly, until the onion is soft.

3 Add the tomatoes, dates, currants and stock. Bring to the boil, return the chicken to the pan, cover with sauce, lower the heat and simmer uncovered for 30 minutes. Add the lemon zest and season to taste. Bring back to the boil and boil for 5 minutes, or until thickened. Garnish with almonds and parsley and serve with buttered rice.

NUTRITION PER SERVE
Protein 56 g; Fat 20 g; Carbohydrate 17 g; Dietary Fibre 3.5 g; Cholesterol 175 mg; 1975 kJ (470 Cal)

An easy way to coat the chicken with flour is to toss them both in a bag.

Brown the chicken on all sides, turning it regularly to prevent sticking.

Add the tomatoes, dates, currants and stock to the softened onion.

HUNGARIAN VEAL GOULASH

Preparation time: 20 minutes
Total cooking time: 2 hours
Serves 4

2 tablespoons olive oil
2 medium onions, chopped
500 g (1 lb 2 oz) stewing veal, cubed
1 tablespoon Hungarian paprika
1/4 teaspoon caraway seeds
425 g (15 oz) can chopped tomatoes
500 ml (2 cups) beef stock
1 large potato, diced
1 large carrot, sliced
1 green capsicum (pepper), chopped
125 g (1/2 cup) sour cream

1 Heat the oil in a large heavy-based pan. Fry the onion for 10 minutes, stirring often, until soft and golden brown. Remove the onion, increase the heat and brown the veal in batches. Return the veal and onion to the pan.

2 Add the paprika, caraway seeds, tomatoes and stock. Bring to the boil, reduce the heat, cover and simmer for 1 1/4 hours.

3 Add the diced potato, carrot and capsicum and cook, uncovered, for 20 minutes, or until the vegetables are tender. Season to taste with salt and freshly ground black pepper, then stir in the sour cream. Serve with rice or pasta.

NUTRITION PER SERVE
Protein 30 g; Fat 25 g; Carbohydrate 15 g; Dietary Fibre 4 g; Cholesterol 145 mg; 1690 kJ (405 Cal)

Brown the meat in small batches so that it browns but doesn't stew in the liquid.

Stir in the paprika, caraway seeds, undrained tomatoes and stock.

Add the potato, carrot and capsicum for the last 20 minutes of cooking.

Use the prawn shells and trimmings to make a good base stock.

Use a slotted spoon to lift the sausage from the oil in the pan.

Add the canned tomatoes and their juice to the pan with the herbs.

After 25 minutes the rice should have absorbed most of the liquid.

SEAFOOD JAMBALAYA

Preparation time: 20 minutes
Total cooking time: 1 hour 10 minutes
Serves 6

1 kg (2 lb 4 oz) raw king prawns (shrimp)
1 small onion, chopped
1 stick celery, chopped
250 ml (1 cup) dry white wine
60 ml (1/4 cup) vegetable oil
200 g (7 oz) spicy sausage, chopped
1 medium onion, chopped
1 red capsicum (pepper), chopped
1 stick celery, chopped
425 g (15 oz) can crushed tomatoes
1/2 teaspoon cayenne pepper
1/2 teaspoon cracked black pepper
1/4 teaspoon dried thyme
1/4 teaspoon dried oregano
400 g (2 cups) long-grain rice

1 Shell the prawns, remove the back veins and set the prawns aside. Put the trimmings in a pan with the small onion, celery, wine and 1 litre (4 cups) of water. Bring to the boil, then reduce the heat and simmer for 20 minutes. Strain, reserving the stock.

2 Heat the oil in a large heavy-based pan and cook the sausage for 5 minutes, until browned. Remove from the pan and set aside.

3 Add the onion, capsicum and celery to the pan and cook, stirring often, for 5 minutes. Add the tomato, pepper and herbs, bring to the boil and then reduce the heat to simmer, covered, for 10 minutes.

4 Return the sausage to the pan and add the rice and prawn stock. Bring back to the boil, reduce the heat and simmer, covered, for 25 minutes, until almost all the liquid has been absorbed and the rice is tender. Add the prawns, cover and cook for 5 minutes. Serve immediately.

NUTRITION PER SERVE
Protein 45 g; Fat 20 g; Carbohydrate 60 g; Dietary Fibre 4 g; Cholesterol 265 mg; 2565 kJ (612 Cal)

PORK AND APPLE BRAISE

Preparation time: 20 minutes
Total cooking time: 40 minutes
Serves 4

2 tablespoons oil
1 large onion, thinly sliced
1 garlic clove, chopped
2 teaspoons soft brown sugar
2 green apples, cut into wedges
4 pork loin steaks or medallions
2 tablespoons brandy
2 tablespoons seeded mustard
250 ml (1 cup) rich chicken stock
110 g (1/2 cup) pitted prunes
185 ml (3/4 cup) cream

1 Heat the oil in a large heavy-based pan. Cook the onion and garlic for 10 minutes over low heat, stirring often, until softened and golden brown. Add the sugar and apple and cook, stirring regularly, until the apple begins to brown. Remove from the pan.

2 Reheat the pan and lightly brown the pork steaks, two at a time; return to the pan. Add the brandy and stir until it has nearly all evaporated. Add the mustard and stock. Simmer over low heat, covered, for 15 minutes.

3 Return the apple to the pan with the prunes and cream and simmer for 10 minutes, or until the pork is tender. Season to taste before serving.

NUTRITION PER SERVE
Protein 25 g; Fat 12 g; Carbohydrate 22 g; Dietary Fibre 4 g; Cholesterol 55 mg; 1250 kJ (298 Cal)

COOK'S FILE

Hint: Take care not to overcook pork or it can become tough and dry.

Stir the apple regularly over the heat until it begins to brown.

Brown the pork steaks two at a time and then return them all to the pan.

Put the browned apple back in the pan with the prunes and cream.

VEGETABLE STEW WITH COUSCOUS

Preparation time: 30 minutes
Total cooking time: 40 minutes
Serves 4

2 tablespoons olive oil
1 onion, sliced
2 teaspoons mustard seeds
2 teaspoons ground cumin
1 teaspoon paprika
1 garlic clove, crushed
2 teaspoons grated ginger
2 sticks celery, thickly sliced
2 small carrots, thickly sliced
2 small parsnips, peeled, cubed
300 g (10½ oz) pumpkin, diced
2 zucchini (courgettes), sliced
375 ml (1½ cups) vegetable stock
185 g (1 cup) instant couscous
30 g (1 oz) butter

1 Heat the oil in a large pan. Add the onion and cook over medium heat for 10 minutes, until very soft and lightly golden, stirring occasionally. Add the mustard seeds, spices, garlic and ginger and stir for 1 minute. Add the vegetables and stir to coat with spices.

2 Add the stock and bring to the boil. Reduce the heat and simmer, partially covered, for 30 minutes, until tender.

3 Put the couscous in a heatproof bowl. Add 185 ml (¾ cup) of boiling water and stand for 2 minutes. Add the butter and stir until melted, then fluff up the grains with a fork. Serve with the vegetables.

NUTRITION PER SERVE
Protein 9 g; Fat 16 g; Carbohydrate 60 g; Dietary Fibre 6 g; Cholesterol 20 mg; 2766 kJ (655 Cal)

Add the mustard seeds, cumin, paprika, garlic and ginger.

Simmer until the vegetables are tender but not breaking up.

Separate the grains of couscous and fluff them up with a fork.

FAMOUS IRISH STEW

Preparation time: 20 minutes
Total cooking time: 1 hour 15 minutes
Serves 4

8 lamb neck chops
4 thick rashers bacon
30 g (1 oz) dripping or butter
1 kg (2 lb 4 oz) potatoes, sliced
3 carrots, sliced
3 medium onions, thickly sliced
500 ml (2 cups) beef stock
4 thyme sprigs

1 Trim the chops, removing any excess fat, and cut the bacon into short strips. Heat the dripping or butter in a pan and cook the chops until brown on both sides; remove from the pan. Add the bacon and cook until crisp. Remove from the pan and leave to drain on paper towels.

2 Arrange half the potato, carrot and onion in the base of a deep, heavy-based pan. Season with pepper and add half the bacon. Layer the chops over this and cover with the rest of the potato, carrot, onion and bacon.

3 Add the stock and thyme. Cover, bring to the boil, reduce the heat and simmer for 1 hour, or until the lamb is very tender.

NUTRITION PER SERVE
Protein 40 g; Fat 15 g; Carbohydrate 40 g; Dietary Fibre 7 g; Cholesterol 110 mg; 1865 kJ (445 Cal)

COOK'S FILE

Note: Traditionally, Irish Stew was made from mutton with no potatoes or carrots. The addition of vegetables makes the dish a satisfying one-pot meal. Try using lemon thyme for a slightly different flavour.

Use a sharp knife to remove any excess fat from the chops.

Spread the chops in one layer over the vegetables and bacon.

Once all the ingredients are layered, pour the stock and thyme over them.

VEAL BRAISED WITH LEMON THYME

Preparation time: 15 minutes
Total cooking time: 1 hour 30 minutes
Serves 4

2 tablespoons olive oil
one 6 cutlet rack of veal, trimmed to a neat shape
2 medium leeks, finely sliced
30 g (1 oz) butter
1 tablespoon plain (all-purpose) flour
1 tablespoon grated lemon zest
500 ml (2 cups) chicken stock
375 ml (1$^1/_2$ cups) white wine
2 tablespoons fresh lemon thyme leaves
125 ml ($^1/_2$ cup) cream

1 Heat the oil in a deep heavy-based frying pan over medium heat and brown the veal well on all sides then remove from the pan. Add the leeks and butter to the pan, reduce the heat and cover. Simmer for 10 minutes, stirring occasionally. Be careful not to burn the leeks or they will be bitter.

2 Add the flour to the pan and stir continuously for 2 minutes. Add the zest and a little pepper, stir in the stock and wine and bring to the boil, stirring continuously. Reduce the heat.

3 Return the veal to the pan, with any juices. Cover and simmer for 1 hour, or until the veal is tender. Cut the veal into cutlets. Add the thyme, cream and salt to the sauce. Serve over the veal.

NUTRITION PER SERVE
Protein 30 g; Fat 32 g; Carbohydrate 5 g; Dietary Fibre 2 g; Cholesterol 160 mg; 2010 kJ (480 Cal)

Remove the fat and trim the veal rack into a neat shape.

Add the grated lemon zest to the leeks in the pan.

Put the browned veal back in the pan once you have braised the leeks.

Famous Irish Stew (top) and Veal Braised with Lemon Thyme

COQ AU VIN

Preparation time: 20 minutes
Total cooking time: 1 hour
Serves 6

plain (all-purpose) flour
2 kg (4 lb 8 oz) chicken pieces
3 tablespoons oil
4 thick bacon rashers, sliced
12 small pickling onions
2 garlic cloves, crushed
2 tablespoons brandy
375 ml (1 1/2 cups) good red wine
375 ml (1 1/2 cups) chicken stock
2 bay leaves
1 fresh bouquet garni
3 tablespoons tomato paste (purée)
250 g (9 oz) small button mushrooms

1 Season the flour with a little salt and pepper and coat the chicken; shake off any excess flour. Heat 2 tablespoons of the oil in a heavy-based pan and brown the chicken in small batches; drain on paper towels.
2 Heat the remaining oil in the cleaned pan. Add the bacon, onions and garlic and cook, stirring, until the onions are browned. Add the chicken, brandy, wine, stock, bay leaves, bouquet garni and tomato paste. Bring to the boil, reduce the heat and simmer, covered, for 30 minutes.
3 Add the mushrooms, stirring to combine, and simmer, uncovered, for 10 minutes, until the chicken is tender and the sauce has slightly thickened. Serve with crusty French bread.

NUTRITION PER SERVE
Protein 60 g; Fat 22 g; Carbohydrate 8 g; Dietary Fibre 2 g; Cholesterol 185 mg; 2175 kJ (520 Cal)

Wrap some fresh herbs in muslin to make a bouquet garni.

Brown the chicken well and drain on paper towels.

Add the chicken, brandy, wine, stock, bouquet garni and tomato paste.

BEEF STEW WITH PECANS

Preparation time: 15 minutes
Total cooking time: 2 hours
Serves 4

60 ml (1/4 cup) olive oil
1 onion, sliced
120 g (4 1/4 oz) mushrooms, sliced
1–2 garlic cloves, crushed
1 1/2 tablespoons plain (all-purpose) flour
1 teaspoon ground cinnamon
1 1/2 teaspoons salt
1/2 teaspoon black pepper
1/2 teaspoon ground nutmeg
1/2 teaspoon ground coriander
pinch cayenne pepper
1 teaspoon grated ginger
750 g (1 lb 10 oz) lean stewing beef, cubed
185 ml (3/4 cup) beef stock
60 ml (1/4 cup) red wine
1 tablespoon soy sauce
12 prunes, pitted, soaked in 125 ml (1/2 cup) beef stock
1 tablespoon soft brown sugar
60 g (2 1/4 oz) pecan nuts

1 Heat half the oil in a large pan. Fry the onion for 3 minutes until soft, add the mushrooms and garlic and cook for 2 minutes. Remove from the pan. Combine the flour, half the cinnamon, 1 teaspoon salt, spices and ginger, then coat the meat. Add the remaining oil to the pan and brown the meat in batches. Remove from the pan.

2 Add the stock, wine, soy sauce and extra stock (from the prunes) to the pan. Bring to the boil, return the onions, mushrooms, garlic and meat to the pan. Simmer for 2 hours. Add the sugar and cook for 10 minutes, or until the meat is tender.

3 Heat the remaining oil in a small pan and fry the pecans for 4 minutes, or until golden brown. Add the rest of the salt and cinnamon and toss to coat the pecans. Add these to the stew with the prunes 5 minutes before serving.

NUTRITION PER SERVE
Protein 45 g; Fat 35 g; Carbohydrate 20 g; Dietary Fibre 6 g; Cholesterol 100 mg; 2452 kJ (585 Cal)

To coat the meat toss it in a plastic bag with the seasoned flour.

Return the onions, mushrooms, garlic and meat to the pan.

Make sure the pecans are well coated with the cinnamon and salt.

LAMB CHOP CASSEROLE

Preparation time: 15 minutes
Total cooking time: 1 hour 15 minutes
Serves 4

6–8 lamb chump chops
1 teaspoon oil
1 large onion, finely chopped
105 g (1/3 cup) redcurrant jelly
1 teaspoon grated lemon zest
1 tablespoon lemon juice
1 tablespoon barbecue sauce
1 tablespoon tomato sauce
125 ml (1/2 cup) chicken stock

1 Trim any fat from the lamb. Preheat the oven to 170°C (325°F/Gas 3). Heat the oil in a large heavy-based frying pan; add the chops and cook over medium-high heat for 3 minutes, turning once, until well browned. Transfer to a casserole dish.

2 Add the onion to the frying pan and cook over medium heat, stirring frequently, for 5 minutes or until the onion is softened. Add the jelly, lemon zest and juice, barbecue and tomato sauces and stock. Stir for 2–3 minutes until heated through. Pour over the chops and stir well, cover and place in the oven. Cook for 1 hour, or until the meat is tender, turning 2–3 times. Lift out the chops onto a side plate and leave them to keep warm.

3 Pour the sauce into a pan and boil rapidly for 5 minutes until the sauce has thickened and reduced. Return the chops to the sauce before serving.

NUTRITION PER SERVE
Protein 30 g; Fat 11 g; Carbohydrate 13 g; Dietary Fibre 1 g; Cholesterol 95 mg; 1150 kJ (275 Cal)

COOK'S FILE

Storage time: Keep covered and refrigerated for up to 2 days. Suitable to freeze for up to 1 month.

Once the chops have been well browned put them in a casserole dish.

Pour the sauce over the chops in the dish and stir to combine.

Use a pair of tongs to turn the chops a couple of times during cooking.

VEGETARIAN CHILLI

Preparation time: 15 minutes
Total cooking time: 40 minutes
Serves 6–8

130 g (3/4 cup) burghul (cracked wheat)
2 tablespoons olive oil
1 large onion, finely chopped
2 garlic cloves, crushed
1 teaspoon chilli powder
2 teaspoons ground cumin
1 teaspoon cayenne pepper
1/2 teaspoon ground cinnamon
2 x 400 g (14 oz) cans crushed tomatoes
750 ml (3 cups) vegetable stock
440 g (15 1/2 oz) can red kidney beans, rinsed and drained
2 x 300 g (10 1/2 oz) cans chickpeas, rinsed and drained
310 g (10 3/4 oz) can corn kernels, drained
2 tablespoons tomato paste (purée)
corn chips and sour cream

1 Soak the burghul in 250 ml (1 cup) of hot water for 10 minutes. Heat the oil in a large heavy-based pan and cook the onion for 10 minutes, stirring often, until soft and golden.

2 Add the garlic, chilli powder, cumin, cayenne and cinnamon and cook, stirring, for a further minute.

3 Add the tomatoes, stock and burghul. Bring to the boil and simmer for 10 minutes. Stir in the beans, chickpeas, corn and tomato paste and simmer for 20 minutes, stirring often. Serve with corn chips and sour cream.

NUTRITION PER SERVE (8)
Protein 7 g; Fat 10 g; Carbohydrate 18 g; Dietary Fibre 7 g; Cholesterol 8 mg; 780 kJ (185 Cal)

Stir the garlic and spices into the pan with the onion and cook for a minute.

Add the crushed tomatoes, stock and burghul to the pan.

Stir in the beans, chickpeas, corn kernels and tomato paste.

KASHMIR LAMB WITH SPINACH

Preparation time: 20 minutes
Total cooking time: 1 hour 30 minutes
Serves 4

2 tablespoons oil
750 g (1 lb 10 oz) diced leg of lamb
2 large onions, chopped
3 garlic cloves, crushed
4 cm (1½ inch) fresh ginger, grated
2 teaspoons ground cumin
2 teaspoons ground coriander
2 teaspoons turmeric
¼ teaspoon ground cardamom
¼ teaspoon ground cloves
3 bay leaves
375 ml (1½ cups) chicken stock
125 ml (½ cup) cream
2 bunches English spinach leaves, washed and chopped

1 Heat the oil in a heavy-based pan and brown the lamb in batches, stirring regularly. Remove from the pan. Add the onions, garlic and ginger and cook for 3 minutes, stirring regularly. Add the spices and cook, stirring, for 1–2 minutes or until fragrant. Return the lamb to the pan with any juices. Add the bay leaves and stock.
2 Bring to the boil and then reduce the heat, stir well, cover and simmer for 35 minutes. Add the cream and cook, covered, for a further 20 minutes or until the lamb is very tender.
3 Add the spinach and cook until softened. Season and serve with rice.

NUTRITION PER SERVE
Protein 45 g; Fat 25 g; Carbohydrate 3 g; Dietary Fibre 2 g; Cholesterol 165 mg; 1820 kJ (435 Cal)

COOK'S FILE

Storage time: Curry is best cooked a day in advance and refrigerated. Do not add the spinach until reheating.

Return the browned lamb to the pan and add the bay leaves.

Stir in the cream and simmer until the lamb is very tender.

It will only take a few minutes for the spinach to soften and reduce.

ROMAN CHICKEN

Preparation time: 10 minutes
Total cooking time: 45 minutes
Serves 2–4

1 tablespoon olive oil
1 small onion, sliced
4 thick rashers bacon, diced
4 large or 8 small chicken legs
1 garlic clove, crushed
10 g (⅓ cup) chopped parsley
250 ml (1 cup) chicken stock
1 tablespoon chopped marjoram
440 g (15½ oz) can crushed tomatoes

1 Heat the oil in a large heavy-based pan and cook the onion and bacon over medium heat for 5 minutes. Increase the heat and add the chicken in batches. Brown the chicken on all sides, turning often and taking care not to overcook the onion and bacon, for about 5 minutes.
2 Reduce the heat, add the garlic and parsley and cook for 2–3 minutes. Add the stock and marjoram, stirring well. Add the tomatoes, stir well and season to taste.
3 Bring to the boil, cover the pan and simmer gently for 30 minutes, turning the chicken legs occasionally, until they are cooked through.

NUTRITION PER SERVE (4)
Protein 37 g; Fat 10 g; Carbohydrate 5 g; Dietary Fibre 2 g; Cholesterol 80 mg; 1080 kJ (258 Cal)

Brown the chicken well, taking care not to burn the onion.

Add the stock and marjoram. Stir well to prevent anything sticking to the pan base.

Turn the chicken legs occasionally to ensure even cooking on all sides.

Kashmir Lamb with Spinach (top) and Roman Chicken

OXTAIL RAGOUT

Preparation time: 20 minutes + 3 hours soaking
Total cooking time: 4 hours
Serves 4

1 kg (2 lb 4 oz) oxtail, cut into short pieces (ask your butcher to do this)
30 g (1/4 cup) plain (all-purpose) flour
1 tablespoon ghee or oil
2 rashers bacon, chopped
1 small onion, peeled and studded with 6 whole cloves
2 garlic cloves
2 carrots, quartered lenghways
375 ml (1 1/2 cups) beef or chicken stock
425 g (15 oz) can puréed tomato
1 parsnip, peeled and quartered lengthways
1 leek, thickly sliced

1 Trim any fat from the oxtail and discard. Put the oxtail in a large bowl, cover with water and set aside for 3 hours. Drain and transfer the meat to a large heavy-based pan, cover with fresh water and bring to the boil. Reduce the heat and simmer for 10 minutes, skimming any froth from the surface with a spoon or absorbent paper towel. Drain the meat, allow to cool and pat dry with paper towels.
2 Preheat the oven to 150°C (300°F/Gas 2). Put the flour and a little salt and pepper in a large plastic bag; put the oxtail in the bag and shake to coat with flour. Heat the ghee or oil in a large frying pan, add the bacon and cook over medium heat for 3 minutes, stirring frequently. Remove the bacon from the pan.
3 Add the oxtail and cook, stirring continuously over medium-high heat for 2–3 minutes, or until browned. Transfer to a casserole dish.
4 Add the bacon, onion, garlic and half the carrot. Stir in the stock and tomato purée. Cover and bake for 3 hours. Add the remaining vegetables and cook for 30–40 minutes, or until tender.

NUTRITION PER SERVE
Protein 30 g; Fat 37 g; Carbohydrate 20 g; Dietary Fibre 5 g; Cholesterol 75 mg; 2300 kJ (545 Cal)

Press the cloves firmly into the onion so they don't fall out during cooking.

Put the oxtail in a plastic bag with the flour and shake to coat evenly.

Cook the oxtail over medium-high heat until browned.

Add the remaining carrot with the parsnip and leek.

Use a couple of wooden spoons to toss the lamb cubes in the marinade.

Remove the cardamom pods and cinnamon stick and discard.

Add the marinade and apricot nectar to the meat in the pan.

Add the apricots and prunes and stir through gently.

LAMB AND APRICOT STEW

Preparation time: 30 minutes + marinating
Total cooking time: 1 hour 30 minutes
Serves 4–6

2 kg (4 lb 8 oz) leg lamb, boned (ask your butcher to do this)
1 onion, thickly sliced
125 ml (½ cup) white wine
1 tablespoon grated lemon zest
60 ml (¼ cup) lemon juice
1 tablespoon ground coriander
4 cardamom pods
1 cinnamon stick
salt and freshly ground black pepper
2 tablespoons oil
170 ml (⅔ cup) apricot nectar
90 g (½ cup) dried apricots
110 g (½ cup) pitted prunes
1 tablespoon cornflour (cornstarch)
80 g (½ cup) roasted unsalted cashew nuts
7 g (¼ cup) finely chopped fresh parsley

1 Trim away the skin and excess fat and cut the meat into 3 cm (1¼ inch) cubes. In a large ceramic or glass bowl, combine the onion, wine, lemon zest, juice, coriander, cardamom pods, cinnamon stick, salt and pepper. Toss the lamb in the marinade, cover and refrigerate for at least 8 hours, or overnight. Stir 2 or 3 times.

2 Drain the meat and onion mixture, reserving the marinade, and dry on paper towels. Discard the cardamom and cinnamon. Heat the oil in a large heavy-based frying pan and brown the meat and onion, in batches, over high heat for 2–3 minutes.

3 Return all the meat and onion to the pan; add the marinade and apricot nectar. Bring to the boil, cover with a tight-fitting lid, reduce the heat to low and simmer for 30 minutes; stir once. Stir through the apricots and prunes, cover and simmer for 30 minutes.

4 Mix the cornflour and 1 tablespoon water to a smooth paste. Add to the pan and stir until thickened; simmer for a further 15 minutes, or until the lamb is tender. Scatter with the cashews and parsley and serve with steamed rice.

NUTRITION PER SERVE (6)
Protein 75 g; Fat 23 g; Carbohydrate 19 g; Dietary Fibre 3 g; Cholesterol 210 mg; 2510 kJ (600 Cal)

POACHER'S RABBIT

Preparation time: 30 minutes
Total cooking time: 2 hours 15 minutes
Serves 4

1 tablespoon vinegar
1 tablespoon salt
1 rabbit, about 1 kg (2 lb 4 oz), cut into 12 portions (ask your butcher to do this)
30 g (1/4 cup) plain (all-purpose) flour
salt and freshly ground pepper
80 ml (1/3 cup) olive oil
2 rashers bacon, roughly chopped
8 bulb spring onions, trimmed
2 medium carrots, finely sliced
375 ml (1 1/2 cups) cider
2 teaspoons French mustard
1/2 teaspoon dried rosemary
1/2 teaspoon dried thyme
1 bay leaf
20 g (1/3 cup) finely chopped parsley

1 Add the vinegar and salt to a bowl of water and leave the rabbit portions to soak overnight. Drain, rinse well and dry on paper towels. Combine the flour, salt and pepper in a large bowl and toss in the rabbit portions. Preheat the oven to 180°C (350°F/Gas 4).

2 Heat 60 ml (1/4 cup) of the oil in a large heavy-based frying pan and brown the rabbit portions quickly in batches over medium heat. Transfer to a 2 litre (8 cup) casserole dish.

3 Add the remaining oil to the pan; add the bacon, bulb spring onions and carrot and fry over medium heat for 5 minutes, or until lightly browned. Add to the casserole dish.

4 Pour the cider into the frying pan and stir in the mustard, rosemary, thyme and bay leaf. Bring to the boil and then pour over the rabbit. Cover with a tight-fitting lid and bake for 2 hours, or until tender. Remove the bay leaf and stir in the parsley before serving.

NUTRITION PER SERVE
Protein 65 g; Fat 40 g; Carbohydrate 13 g; Dietary Fibre 2 g; Cholesterol 160 mg; 2864 kJ (684 Cal)

COOK'S FILE

Storage time: Refrigerate for up to 2 days. Freeze for up to 1 month.

Use paper towels to dry the drained and rinsed rabbit portions.

Cut the tops and tails from the bulb spring onions.

Fry the bacon, onions and carrot until lightly browned.

Add the mustard, herbs and bay leaf to the cider in the frying pan.

SAUSAGE CARBONADE

Preparation time: 15 minutes
Total cooking time: 45 minutes
Serves 4–6

750 g (1 lb 10 oz) good quality beef sausages
1 tablespoon olive oil
1 large onion, chopped
2 garlic cloves, chopped
2 teaspoons soft brown sugar
2 tablespoons plain (all-purpose) flour
375 ml (1 1/2 cups) beer
500 ml (2 cups) beef stock
2 bay leaves
2 tablespoons chopped parsley

1 Put the sausages in a pan and cover with cold water. Bring to the boil, reduce the heat and simmer for 5 minutes. Drain and cool.

2 Heat the oil in a large pan, cook the onion and garlic for 5 minutes, stirring regularly. Stir in the sugar and flour for 5–8 minutes over low heat, until the flour is golden brown.

3 Gradually stir in the beer and stock. Add the sausages and bay leaves, bring to the boil, then reduce the heat, cover the pan and simmer for 20 minutes. Remove the bay leaves, stir in the parsley and season.

NUTRITION PER SERVE (6)
Protein 17 g; Fat 32 g; Carbohydrate 9 g; Dietary Fibre 4 g; Cholesterol 70 mg; 1670 kJ (400 Cal)

Put the sausages in a pan with enough cold water to cover them.

Cook the onion and garlic for 5 minutes, stirring regularly.

Lift the bay leaves out of the pan just before serving.

CAJUN SPICED FISH BRAISE

Preparation time: 15 minutes
Total cooking time: 25 minutes
Serves 4

750 g (1 lb 10 oz) ling fillets
2 tablespoons plain (all-purpose) flour
2 tablespoons Cajun spice mix
2 tablespoons olive oil
30 g (1 oz) butter
1 large onion, thickly sliced
1 red capsicum (pepper), sliced
125 ml (1/2 cup) white wine
500 g (2 cups) bottled tomato pasta sauce
1 wide strip lemon zest
8 fresh raw prawns (shrimp), peeled and deveined

1 Cut the fish into bite-sized, thick pieces. Mix the flour and Cajun spice mix together, then lightly coat the fish. Heat the oil and butter in a large heavy-based pan over medium heat. Cook the fish, turning occasionally, until browned on all sides. Remove from the pan.

2 Add the onion and capsicum to the pan and cook, stirring regularly, for 5 minutes. Add the wine and bring to the boil, stirring continuously. Add the tomato pasta sauce and the lemon zest. Bring to the boil, then reduce the heat and simmer for a further 10 minutes.

3 Add the fish and prawns; cook over low heat for 3 minutes, or until the prawns are red and the fish tender and easily flaked with a fork. Remove the zest and season. Serve immediately.

NUTRITION PER SERVE
Protein 43 g; Fat 22 g; Carbohydrate 22 g; Dietary Fibre 4 g; Cholesterol 150 mg; 1995 kJ (477 Cal)

Coat the fish in flour and Cajun spice mix by putting in a bag and shaking.

Cook the fish in the oil and butter until browned on all sides.

When the fish is tender it should be easy to flake with a fork.

Trim any excess fat and sinew from the osso bucco.

Be careful not to leave any white pith on the lemon zest as it will cause bitterness.

Spoon the sauce over the meat in the casserole dish.

Just before you serve, sprinkle the Gremolata over the Osso Bucco.

OSSO BUCCO

Preparation time: 20 minutes
Total cooking time: 2 hours
Serves 4–6

2 tablespoons plain (all-purpose) flour
freshly ground black pepper
6 veal shanks (osso bucco), cut into 4 cm (1 1/2 inch) pieces
1 tablespoon oil
30 g (1 oz) butter
2 garlic cloves, crushed
1 large onion, sliced
2 sticks celery, finely chopped
170 ml (2/3 cup) dry white wine
170 ml (2/3 cup) beef stock
425 g (15 oz) can crushed tomatoes
2 strips lemon zest
3 tablespoons tomato paste (purée)
1/2 teaspoon caster (superfine) sugar

Gremolata
30 g (1/2 cup) chopped parsley
2 garlic cloves, crushed
2 teaspoons grated lemon zest

1 Preheat the oven to 180°C (350°F/Gas 4). Grease a 3 litre (12 cup) casserole dish. Combine the flour and pepper and lightly coat the osso bucco, shaking off any excess.
2 Heat the oil and butter in a pan. Brown the meat quickly on both sides over medium-high heat; drain and transfer to the casserole dish.
3 Add the garlic, onion and celery to the pan and cook, stirring, until just soft. Add the wine, stock, tomatoes, lemon zest, tomato paste and sugar. Bring to the boil, then reduce the heat and simmer for 5 minutes. Spoon the sauce over the meat. Cover and bake for 1 3/4 hours, or until meat is tender.
4 To make the Gremolata: Mix the parsley, garlic and zest. Sprinkle over the Osso Bucco. This is traditionally served with Risotto Milanese, a plain risotto with Parmesan.

NUTRITION PER SERVE **(6)**
Protein 28 g; Fat 9 g; Carbohydrate 9 g; Dietary Fibre 2.5 g; Cholesterol 110 mg; 940 kJ (225 Cal)

CHICKEN AND ORANGE CASSEROLE

Preparation time: 50 minutes
Total cooking time: 1 hour 30 minutes
Serves 4–6

2 small chickens
1 tablespoon olive oil
2 thick rashers bacon, rind removed and thinly sliced
50 g ($1^3/_4$ oz) butter
16 small pickling onions, peeled (ensure ends are intact)
2–3 garlic cloves, crushed
3 teaspoons grated fresh ginger
2 teaspoons grated orange zest
2 teaspoons ground cumin
2 teaspoons ground coriander
2 tablespoons honey
250 ml (1 cup) fresh orange juice
250 ml (1 cup) white wine
125 ml ($^1/_2$ cup) chicken or vegetable stock
1 bunch baby carrots
1 large parsnip, peeled
fresh coriander (cilantro) and orange zest, to serve

1 Using a sharp knife or a pair of kitchen scissors, cut each chicken into 8 pieces discarding the backbone. Remove any excess fat and discard (remove the skin as well, if preferred).

2 Heat about a teaspoon of the oil in a large, deep heavy-based pan. Add the bacon and cook over medium heat for 2–3 minutes, or until just crisp. Remove from the pan and set aside to drain on paper towels. Add the remaining oil and half the butter to the pan. Cook the onions over medium heat until dark golden brown. Shake the pan occasionally to ensure even cooking and browning. Remove from the pan and set aside.

3 Add the chicken pieces to the pan and brown in small batches over medium heat. Remove from the pan and drain on paper towels.

4 Add the remaining butter to the pan. Stir in the garlic, ginger, orange zest, cumin, coriander and honey and cook, stirring, for 1 minute. Add the orange juice, wine and stock to the pan. Bring to the boil and then reduce the heat and simmer for 1 minute. Return the chicken pieces to the pan, cover and leave to simmer over low heat for 40 minutes.

5 Return the onions and bacon to the pan and simmer, covered, for a further 15 minutes. Remove the lid and leave to simmer for a further 15 minutes.

6 Trim the carrots, leaving a little green stalk, and wash well or peel if necessary. Cut the parsnip into small batons. Add the carrots and parsnip to the pan. Cover and cook for 5–10 minutes or until the carrots and parsnip are just tender. Do not overcook the carrots or they will lose their bright colouring. When you are ready to serve, arrange 2–3 chicken pieces on each plate. Put a couple of carrots and a few parsnip batons on top and spoon over a little juice. Garnish with coriander leaves and orange zest.

NUTRITION PER SERVE (6)
Protein 40 g; Fat 18 g; Carbohydrate 22 g; Dietary Fibre 2 g; Cholesterol 145 mg; 1790 kJ (430 Cal)

COOK'S FILE

Storage time: Can be refrigerated for up to 1 day at the end of stage 5. Reheat the casserole gently over low heat and add the carrots and parsnip just prior to serving.

Cut each chicken into 8 even-sized pieces using a knife or pair of scissors.

Cook the pickling onions until they are dark golden brown.

Brown the chicken pieces in batches and drain on paper towels.

Add the orange juice, wine and stock to the pan.

Return the browned pickling onions and cooked bacon to the pan.

Cut the parsnip into batons and leave the stalks on the carrots to provide colour.

HAM, BEAN AND SWEDE CASSEROLE

Preparation time: 35 minutes
Total cooking time: 1 hour 45 minutes
Serves 4

200 g (1 cup) black-eyed beans, soaked in cold water overnight
1 smoked ham hock
18 small pickling onions
30 g (1 oz) butter
2 tablespoons oil
2 garlic cloves, crushed
2 tablespoons golden syrup
3 teaspoons ground cumin
1 tablespoon German or French mustard
1 swede or turnip, peeled, diced
2 tablespoons tomato paste (purée)

1 Drain the beans and place in a pan. Add the hock and 2 litres (8 cups) water, cover and bring to the boil. Reduce to low; simmer for 30 minutes. Drain, reserving 500 ml (2 cups) of stock. Remove the skin from the hock; chop the meat into bite-sized pieces.

2 Peel the onions, leaving the bases intact. Heat the butter, oil, garlic and syrup in the cleaned pan. Add the onions and cook for 5–10 minutes, or until just starting to turn golden.

3 Stir in the ham, cumin, mustard and swede or turnip and cook for 2 minutes until golden. Season and return the beans to the pan. Add the reserved stock and tomato paste, bring to the boil, reduce the heat and simmer, covered, for 1 hour. Uncover and simmer for 5–10 minutes longer, or until reduced and thickened.

NUTRITION PER SERVE
Protein 20 g; Fat 17 g; Carbohydrate 65 g; Dietary Fibre 11 g; Cholesterol 26 mg; 2140 kJ (510 Cal)

Remove the skin and chop the cooked ham hock into bite-sized pieces.

Peel the onions, leaving the bases intact so that they hold their shape.

Stir in the ham, cumin, mustard and swede or turnip.

PEPPERED VEGETABLE HOTPOT

Preparation time: 30 minutes
Total cooking time: 1 hour 5 minutes
Serves 8–10

2 tablespoons olive oil
2 onions, chopped
2 leeks, washed and chopped
2 garlic cloves, crushed
1.5 litres (6 cups) chicken stock
2 tablespoons chopped fresh rosemary
1–2 teaspoon green peppercorns
4 large potatoes, cubed
2 large turnips, cubed
200 g (7 oz) broccoli, cut into small florets
200 g (7 oz) cauliflower, cut into small florets
155 g (1 cup) fresh or frozen peas

1 Heat the oil in a large heavy-based pan and cook the onion and leek over medium heat for 10 minutes, or until they are tender.

2 Add the garlic and cook for 1 minute further, then add the stock, rosemary, peppercorns and potato to the pan. Bring to the boil and then reduce the heat, cover and leave to simmer for 30 minutes. Add the pieces of turnip and allow to simmer for a further 15 minutes.

3 Add the broccoli, cauliflower and peas and simmer, uncovered, for a further 5 minutes. Season with salt and black pepper to taste.

NUTRITION PER SERVE (10)
Protein 5 g; Fat 4 g; Carbohydrate 14 g; Dietary Fibre 5 g; Cholesterol 0 mg; 465 kJ (110 Cal)

COOK'S FILE

Hint: Serve as a main course with pesto and crusty bread.

Wash the turnips well and roughly chop into large cubes.

Add the stock, rosemary, peppercorns and potato to the pan.

Add the broccoli, cauliflower and peas for the last 5 minutes of cooking.

CHILLI CON CARNE

Preparation time: 10 minutes
Total cooking time: 50 minutes
Serves 4

1 tablespoon olive oil
1 medium onion, chopped
3 garlic cloves, crushed
1 stick celery, sliced
500 g (1 lb 2 oz) lean minced (ground) beef
2 teaspoons chilli powder
pinch cayenne pepper
1 teaspoon dried oregano
440 g (15½ oz) can crushed tomatoes
2 tablespoons tomato paste (purée)
1 teaspoon soft brown sugar
1 tablespoon cider or red wine vinegar
420 g (14½ oz) can red kidney beans, drained

1 Heat the oil in a large pan and add the onion, garlic and celery. Stir over medium heat for 5 minutes, until soft. Add the beef and stir over high heat for 5 minutes, or until well browned.
2 Add the chilli powder, cayenne and oregano to the pan. Stir well and cook for 5 minutes. Add the tomatoes, 125 ml (½ cup) water and the tomato paste and stir well.
3 Simmer, uncovered, for 30 minutes, stirring occasionally. Add the sugar, cider or vinegar and beans. Season with salt and pepper and heat through for 5 minutes. Serve hot with white or brown rice.

NUTRITION PER SERVE
Protein 40 g; Fat 20 g; Carbohydrate 20 g; Dietary Fibre 13 g; Cholesterol 80 mg; 1690 kJ (400 Cal)

COOK'S FILE

Storage time: Keep covered and refrigerated for up to 3 days.

Hint: For a more spicy dish, add some chopped fresh red chillies when you are cooking the onions.

Use a fork to break up any lumps of meat as it browns.

Add the tomatoes, water and tomato paste and stir well.

Add the sugar, cider or vinegar, seasoning and kidney beans and heat through.

NAVARIN OF LAMB

Preparation time: 20 minutes
Total cooking time: 1 hour 45 minutes
Serves 4

1.25 kg (2 lb 12 oz) boned shoulder or leg of lamb (ask your butcher to do this)
30 g (1 oz) butter
1 tablespoon oil
1 small onion, quartered
1 garlic clove, crushed
2 rashers bacon, finely chopped
12 small bulb spring onions, stems removed
1 tablespoon plain (all-purpose) flour
250 ml (1 cup) chicken stock
1 tablespoon tomato paste (purée)
1 turnip or swede (rutabaga), peeled and cubed
1 large carrot, thickly sliced
4–6 new potatoes, halved
80 g (1/2 cup) frozen peas

1 Remove any excess fat from the lamb and cut the meat into bite-sized cubes. Preheat the oven to 150°C (300°F/Gas 2). Heat the butter and oil in a heavy-based frying pan. Cook the onion, garlic, bacon and spring onions over medium heat for 5 minutes, or until the onion is soft. Transfer to a large heatproof casserole dish.

2 Add the lamb to the frying pan and brown quickly in batches; set aside. When all the meat is browned return it to the pan and sprinkle with the flour. Stir for 1 minute to combine, then pour on the stock and tomato paste. Stir until thickened and smooth and pour into the casserole dish.

3 Stir in the turnip or swede, carrot and potato. Cover with a tight-fitting lid and bake for 1 1/2 hours, or until the lamb is tender. Stir 2–3 times during cooking. Add the peas after 1 1/4 hours.

NUTRITION PER SERVE
Protein 9 g; Fat 12 g; Carbohydrate 22 g; Dietary Fibre 7 g; Cholesterol 30 mg; 970 kJ (235 Cal)

COOK'S FILE

Storage time: Keep covered and refrigerated for up to 3 days.

Remove the onion, spring onion, garlic and bacon to a casserole dish.

Return the browned meat to the pan and sprinkle with flour.

Add the turnip, swede, carrot and potato to the meat in the casserole dish.

MINTY LAMB SHANKS

Preparation time: 20 minutes
Total cooking time: 2 hours 10 minutes
Serves 6

6 lamb shanks
1 tablespoon olive oil
1 red onion, finely chopped
2 garlic cloves, crushed
35 g (3/4 cup) chopped mint leaves
1 sprig fresh thyme
2 bay leaves
425 g (15 oz) can crushed tomatoes
500 ml (2 cups) vegetable stock
60 ml (1/4 cup) white wine

1 Preheat the oven to 200°C (400°F/Gas 6). Put the shanks in a baking dish in a single layer, close together. Season. Bake for 20 minutes; turn the shanks, reduce to 180°C (350°F/Gas 4); bake for 20 minutes.
2 Heat the oil in a frying pan. Cook the onion and garlic for 5–8 minutes, or until soft. Stir in 25 g (1/2 cup) of the mint, the thyme and bay leaves. Scatter over the meat, return to the oven and cook for 15 minutes.
3 Combine the tomato, stock and wine and pour over the meat. Cover tightly with foil or a lid and bake for 1 1/4 hours. Garnish with the remaining mint and serve with pasta. Best made a day or two in advance and refrigerated.

NUTRITION PER SERVE
Protein 30 g; Fat 6 g; Carbohydrate 4 g; Dietary Fibre 2 g; Cholesterol 85mg; 815 kJ (195 Cal)

Put the shanks in one layer, close together and season with salt and pepper.

Once the onion is soft, stir in the thyme, bay leaves and mint.

Mix together the tomato, stock and wine and pour over the lamb shanks.

CHICKEN AND COCONUT CREAM CURRY

Preparation time: 20 minutes
Total cooking time: 50 minutes
Serves 4

1.5 kg (3 lb 5 oz) chicken thigh fillets, trimmed of fat
1 tablespoon vegetable oil
400 ml (14 fl oz) coconut cream
2 tablespoons fish sauce
1–2 small chopped red chillies
4 coriander (cilantro) roots, chopped, leaves reserved
1 lemon grass, chopped finely
6 pieces dried galangal
6 dried makrut (kaffir) lime leaves
1 tablespoon red curry paste
2 teaspoons soft brown sugar
1 tablespoon lemon juice
2 small zucchini (courgettes), thickly sliced
80 g (1/2 cup) green peas

1 Cut the chicken into bite-sized pieces and pat dry with paper towels. Heat the oil in a frying pan and brown the chicken in batches. Set aside.
2 Combine the coconut cream, fish sauce, chilli, coriander root, lemon grass, galangal and lime leaves in a large pan. Bring to the boil, stirring, then reduce the heat; add the chicken. Simmer for 30 minutes, or until the chicken is tender, stirring often.
3 Add the curry paste, sugar and lemon juice and stir well. Stir in the zucchini and peas and simmer for a further 5 minutes, until the vegetables are just tender. Remove the galangal and lime leaves to serve.

NUTRITION PER SERVE
Protein 70 g; Fat 33 g; Carbohydrate 10 g; Dietary Fibre 3 g; Cholesterol 150 mg; 2587 kJ (620 Cal)

Lemon grass, makrut (kaffir) lime leaves and galangal are available at Asian stores.

Reduce the heat and return the browned chicken to the pan.

Use a pair of tongs to lift out and discard the galangal and lime leaves.

Minty Lamb Shanks (top) and Chicken and Coconut Cream Curry

CIOPPINO

Preparation time: 20 minutes
Total cooking time: 55 minutes
Serves 4

1 kg (2 lb 4 oz) firm white-fleshed fish fillets, skinned and boned
375 g (13 oz) raw king prawns (shrimp)
1 raw lobster tail, in shell
12 fresh mussels
2 dried mushrooms
60 ml (1/4 cup) olive oil
1 large onion, finely chopped
1 green capsicum (pepper), chopped
2–3 garlic cloves, crushed
425 g (15 oz) can crushed tomatoes
250 ml (1 cup) white wine
250 ml (1 cup) tomato juice
250 ml (1 cup) fish stock or water
bay leaf
2 sprigs parsley
6 basil leaves, chopped
60 g (1 cup) chopped parsley

1 Cut the fish into bite-size pieces. Remove the heads and shells from the prawns, leaving tails intact, then devein. Remove lobster meat from the shell and cut into small pieces. (Make your own stock by simmering the fish, lobster and prawn trimmings in water for 5 minutes, then strain.) Scrub the mussels and remove their beards. Discard any open mussels, then soak the rest in cold water for 10 minutes. Soak the mushrooms in water for 20 minutes, squeeze dry and chop finely.

2 Heat the oil in a pan; cook the onion, capsicum and garlic for 5 minutes, or until soft. Add the mushrooms, tomato, wine, tomato juice, stock, bay leaf and herbs. Bring to the boil, then simmer for 30 minutes.

3 Layer the fish and prawns in a large pan, add the sauce, cover and leave on a low heat for 10 minutes, until prawns are pink and fish is cooked. Add the lobster and mussels; simmer for 2–3 minutes. Discard any unopened mussels. Sprinkle with parsley.

NUTRITION PER SERVE
Protein 85 g; Fat 25 g; Carbohydrate 9 g; Dietary Fibre 3 g; Cholesterol 350 mg; 2885 kJ (687 Cal)

Remove the heads and shells from the prawns but leave the tails intact.

To remove the lobster shell, cut the shell on the softer, white underside.

Scrub the mussels well and remove their beards. Discard any open mussels.

Squeeze the mushrooms gently to get rid of the excess liquid.

MEXICAN BEEF STEW

Preparation time: 30 minutes
Total cooking time: 1 hour 30 minutes
Serves 6

500 g (1 lb 2 oz) Roma (plum) tomatoes, halved
6 flour tortillas
1–2 red chillies, finely chopped
1 tablespoon olive oil
1 kg (2 lb 4 oz) stewing beef, cubed
1/2 teaspoon black pepper
2 onions, thinly sliced
375 ml (1 1/2 cups) beef stock
3 tablespoons tomato paste (purée)
375 g (13 oz) can kidney beans, drained
1 teaspoon chilli powder
125 g (1/2 cup) sour cream

1 Preheat the oven to 180°C (350°F/ Gas 4). Grill (broil) the tomatoes, skin side up for 6–8 minutes, or until the skin is black and blistered. Cool, remove the skin and roughly chop the flesh.
2 Bake 2 of the tortillas for 4 minutes, or until crisp. Break into pieces, put in a food processor with the tomato and chilli and process until almost smooth.
3 Heat the oil in a pan. Brown the beef in batches, then remove. Add the onion to the pan; cook for 5 minutes. Return the meat to the pan. Stir in the tomato mixture, stock and tomato paste and bring to the boil. Reduce the heat, cover and simmer for 1 1/4 hours. Add the beans and chilli powder.
4 Grill the remaining tortillas for 3 minutes each side; cool, cut in wedges. Serve with the stew and sour cream.

NUTRITION PER SERVE
Protein 50 g; Fat 20 g; Carbohydrate 40 g; Dietary Fibre 8 g; Cholesterol 125 mg; 2235 kJ (535 Cal)

Grill the tomatoes until the skin is black and blistered and it will peel away easily.

Once the tortillas are crisp, break into pieces and put in the food processor.

Stir in the processed mixture, stock and tomato paste.

CHICKEN CACCIATORE

Preparation time: 20 minutes
Total cooking time: 1 hour 15 minutes
Serves 4–6

1 tablespoon olive oil
1 kg (2 lb 4 oz) chicken pieces
2 tablespoons plain (all-purpose) flour
1 large onion, finely chopped
2 garlic cloves, chopped
2 x 425 g (15 oz) cans tomatoes
500 ml (2 cups) chicken stock
125 ml (1/2 cup) white wine
2 tablespoons tomato paste (purée)
1 teaspoon caster (superfine) sugar
45 g (1/4 cup) black olives
2 tablespoons chopped basil
2 tablespoons chopped parsley

1 Heat the oil in a large heavy-based pan. Brown the chicken in batches over medium heat. Remove from the pan and sprinkle with flour.

2 Add the onion and garlic to the pan and cook for 10 minutes over low heat, stirring occasionally. Add the tomatoes and their juice, the chicken stock and wine. Bring to the boil and then reduce the heat and simmer for 15 minutes. Add the tomato paste, sugar and chicken and stir well.

3 Cover and simmer for 30 minutes over low heat. Add the olives, basil and parsley, then season with salt and pepper and simmer for 15 minutes, stirring occasionally.

NUTRITION PER SERVE (6)
Protein 30 g; Fat 10 g; Carbohydrate 10 g; Dietary Fibre 3 g; Cholesterol 90 mg; 1100 kJ (265 Cal)

Remove the browned chicken from the pan and sprinkle with flour.

Add the chicken pieces, tomato paste and sugar to the pan.

Stir in the olives, basil and parsley and taste to check on the seasoning.

MEDITERRANEAN VEGETABLE POT

Preparation time: 20 minutes
Total cooking time: 40 minutes
Serves 4

60 ml (1/4 cup) olive oil
1 onion, chopped
2 garlic cloves, crushed
1 red and 1 green capsicum (pepper), chopped
3 slender eggplants (aubergines), sliced
3 zucchini (courgettes), sliced
400 g (2 cups) long-grain rice
100 g (3 1/2 oz) button mushrooms, sliced
750 ml (3 cups) chicken stock
250 ml (1 cup) white wine
400 g (14 oz) can crushed tomatoes
2 tablespoons tomato paste (purée)
150 g (5 1/2 oz) feta cheese

1 Heat the oil in a pan and cook the onion over medium heat for 10 minutes until very soft but not brown. Add the garlic and cook for a further minute.
2 Add the capsicum, stir for 3 minutes. Add the eggplant and zucchini and stir for 5 minutes, then add the rice, stirring for 2 minutes.
3 Stir in the mushrooms, stock, wine, tomatoes and paste until combined. Bring to the boil, reduce the heat, cover and simmer for 20 minutes—rice should absorb most of the liquid. Serve topped with crumbled feta.

NUTRITION PER SERVE
Protein 20 g; Fat 25 g; Carbohydrate 92 g; Dietary Fibre 9 g; Cholesterol 25 mg; 2980 kJ (710 Cal)

Cook the onion until it is very soft but not browned.

Add the zucchini and eggplant to the pan and stir-fry a little longer.

Add the mushrooms, stock, wine, crushed tomatoes and tomato paste.

LANCASHIRE HOTPOT

Preparation time: 20 minutes
Total cooking time: 2 hours
Serves 8

8 forequarter chops, cut 2.5 cm (1 inch) thick
4 lamb kidneys, cut in quarters, cores removed
50 g (1¾ oz) dripping or butter
30 g (¼ cup) plain (all-purpose) flour
4 medium potatoes, thinly sliced
2 large brown onions, sliced
2 sticks celery, chopped
1 large carrot, chopped
435 ml (1¾ cups) chicken or beef stock
200 g (7 oz) button mushrooms, sliced
2 teaspoons chopped fresh thyme
1 tablespoon Worcestershire sauce

1 Preheat the oven to 160°C (315°F/ Gas 2–3). Grease a large casserole dish. Trim the meat of excess fat and sinew and toss the chops and kidneys in flour, shaking off the excess. Heat the dripping in a frying pan and brown the chops quickly on both sides. Remove from the pan and brown the kidneys. Layer half the potato slices in the base of the dish and place the chops and kidneys on top of them.
2 Add the onion, celery and carrot to the pan and cook until the carrot begins to brown. Layer on top of the meat. Sprinkle the remaining flour over the base of the pan and cook, stirring, until dark brown. Pour in the stock and bring to the boil, stirring. Add the mushrooms, thyme and Worcestershire sauce, reduce the heat, season and simmer for 10 minutes. Pour into the casserole dish.
3 Layer the remaining potato over the top of the casserole, to cover the meat and vegetables. Cover and bake for 1¼ hours. Remove the lid and cook for a further 30 minutes, or until the potatoes are brown.

NUTRITION PER SERVE
Protein 40 g; Fat 10 g; Carbohydrate 11 g; Dietary Fibre 3 g; Cholesterol 170 mg; 1227 kJ (295 Cal)

Brown the kidneys in the hot dripping or butter, stirring regularly.

Stir in the mushrooms, seasoning, herbs and Worcestershire sauce.

Layer the remaining potato over the top of the casserole.

GAME CASSEROLE

Preparation time: 30 minutes
Total cooking time: 2 hours
Serves 6

1 kg (2 lb 4 oz) venison shoulder
2 tablespoons oil
3 rashers bacon, chopped
3 medium onions, thickly sliced
2 tablespoons plain (all-purpose) flour
250 ml (1 cup) red wine
125 ml (1/2 cup) chicken stock
2 tablespoons port
2 medium carrots, chopped
1 stick celery, chopped
1 garlic clove, crushed
1 bay leaf
1 cinnamon stick
2 cloves
1/2 teaspoon ground nutmeg
1/2 teaspoon dried thyme
1/2 teaspoon chopped chilli
150 g (5 1/2 oz) button mushrooms, cut in half

1 Preheat the oven to 180°C (350°F/Gas 4). Trim the excess fat and sinew from the venison and cut into cubes. Heat half the oil in a large pan, add the bacon and fry over medium heat until brown. Remove. Add the onion and cook until soft and golden. Remove and set aside.

2 Add the remaining oil to the pan. Brown the venison in small batches, return all to the pan, sprinkle the flour and cook, stirring, for 1 minute. Remove from the heat and stir in the wine, stock, port, bacon, onion, carrot, celery, garlic, bay leaf, cinnamon, cloves, nutmeg, thyme and chilli.

3 Pour into a casserole dish, cover and bake for 1 1/2 hours. Add the mushrooms, then cook for 30 minutes.

NUTRITION PER SERVE
Protein 40 g; Fat 15 g; Carbohydrate 9 g; Dietary Fibre 3 g; Cholesterol 105 mg; 1550 kJ (370 Cal)

Cook the onion slices until they are soft and golden.

Return all the browned venison to the pan and sprinkle with flour.

Add the mushrooms to the casserole and cook for a further 30 minutes.

BEEF OLIVES

Beef olives can be filled with the traditional sage filling or the sun-dried tomato filling below. Each filling will serve 4 people.

Preparation time: 20 minutes
Total cooking time: 1hour 30 minutes
Serves 4

1 kg (2 lb 4 oz) skirt steak, cut into thin slices lengthways
30 g (1/4 cup) plain (all-purpose) flour
1 tablespoon olive oil
1 carrot, finely chopped
250 ml (1 cup) red wine
425 g (15 oz) can crushed tomatoes
2 bay leaves

Traditional sage filling:
1 tablespoon olive oil
1 small onion, chopped
2 garlic cloves, chopped
2 large tomatoes, diced
40 g (1/2 cup) fresh breadcrumbs
2 tablespoons chopped sage

Sun-dried tomato, mushroom and olive filling:
1 tablespoon olive oil
4 spring onions (scallions), chopped
2 garlic cloves, crushed
100 g (31/2 oz) mushrooms, chopped
8 sun-dried (sun-blushed) tomatoes, chopped
60 g (21/4 oz) black olives, chopped
40 g (1/2 cup) fresh breadcrumbs
2 tablespoons chopped basil

1 Put the steak between sheets of plastic wrap and pound with a meat mallet until very thin, taking care not to tear the meat. Set aside.

2 To make the Sage Filling: Heat the oil in a deep heavy-based pan and cook the onion and garlic, stirring, for 3 minutes. Transfer the mixture to a bowl; mix in the tomato, breadcrumbs and sage, then season. Set aside.

To make the Sun-dried Tomato Filling: Heat the oil in a heavy-based pan, add the spring onion, garlic and mushrooms and cook for 3 minutes, stirring continuously, over medium heat. Transfer to a bowl, add the tomatoes, olives, breadcrumbs, basil and salt and pepper, to taste. Mix well and set aside.

3 Lay a slice of meat on a board and place about 1/3 cup of filling neatly along the short edge. Roll up firmly, folding in a little of the sides as you roll, and tie with string to secure.

4 Repeat with the remaining meat and filling. Roll the Beef Olives lightly in flour, shaking off any excess.

5 Wipe out the pan with paper towels and add the oil. Brown the carrots and Beef Olives in batches over medium heat, turning regularly, and then return them all to the pan.

6 Add the wine, undrained tomatoes and bay leaves to the pan and turn the Olives to coat them. Cover and simmer very gently over low heat for 1 hour, or until tender. Remove from the sauce, trim away the string and slice the Olives. Remove the bay leaves and purée the sauce in a food processor or blender until smooth. Serve poured over the Beef Olives.

NUTRITION PER SERVE
Protein 65 g; Fat 25 g; Carbohydrate 30 g; Dietary Fibre 6.5 g; Cholesterol 170 mg; 2695 kJ (645 Cal)

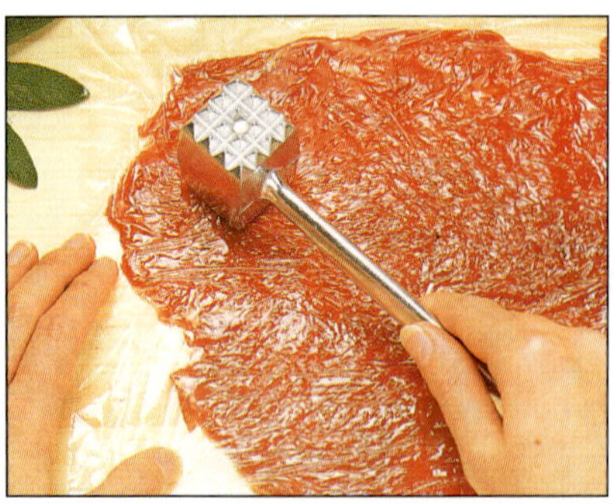

Pound the steak with a meat mallet between two sheets of plastic wrap.

For the Sage Filling add the breadcrumbs with the other ingredients and mix well.

Roll the Olives firmly, folding in a little from the sides as you roll.

Once they are rolled up, secure the Olives with string.

Brown the Olives in batches and then return them all to the pan.

Use a pair of tongs to lift the Beef Olives from the sauce.

CHICKPEA AND VEGETABLE CURRY

Preparation time: 30 minutes
Total cooking time: 35 minutes
Serves 4

1 tablespoon oil
1 onion, chopped
1 tablespoon grated fresh ginger
3 garlic cloves, crushed
1/2 teaspoon fennel seeds
2 teaspoons curry powder
1 teaspoon finely chopped chilli, optional
400 ml (14 fl oz) coconut milk
425 g (15 oz) chickpeas, drained
3 zucchini (courgettes), chopped
200 g (7 oz) orange sweet potato, chopped
150 g (5 1/2 oz) green beans, chopped
200 g (7 oz) broccoli, cut into small florets
20 g (1/3 cup) shredded coconut

1 Heat the oil in a large heavy-based pan and cook the onion over medium heat for about 10 minutes, or until soft and golden. Add the ginger, garlic, fennel seeds, curry powder and chilli (if using). Cook, stirring, for 2 minutes, or until fragrant.

2 Stir in the coconut milk, chickpeas, zucchini, orange sweet potato, beans and broccoli florets and bring to the boil. Reduce the heat, cover and leave to simmer for 20 minutes, or until the vegetables are tender.

3 Preheat the oven to 180°C (350°F/Gas 4). Spread the shredded coconut on a large baking tray and toast in the oven for a few minutes until lightly golden. Serve over the curry as a garnish.

NUTRITION PER SERVE
Protein 15 g; Fat 30 g; Carbohydrate 30 g; Dietary Fibre 14 g; Cholesterol 0 mg; 1955 kJ (465 Cal)

Add the ginger, garlic and spices and cook until fragrant.

Add the drained chickpeas to the pan with the other vegetables.

Spread the coconut on a baking tray and toast until lightly golden.

LAMB AND WHITE BEAN CASSEROLE

Preparation time: 20 minutes + overnight soaking
Total cooking time: 2 hours 45 minutes
Serves 4

150 g (3/4 cup) dried cannellini beans
1 kg (2 lb 4 oz) lamb neck chops
1 tablespoon oil
2 onions, chopped
3 garlic cloves, crushed
800 g (1 lb 12 oz) can crushed tomatoes
1 tablespoon sugar
1/2 teaspoon chopped chilli
125 ml (1/2 cup) chicken stock
2 tablespoons white wine vinegar
large sprig fresh rosemary
1 tablespoon lemon juice
1 teaspoon finely grated lemon zest

1 Place the beans in a large bowl, cover them with plenty of water and leave to soak overnight.
2 Trim the meat of excess fat and sinew. Heat the oil in a large heavy-based pan and brown the meat in batches. Remove all the meat from the pan and set aside. Add the onion to the pan and cook for 5 minutes until soft and lightly golden. Add the garlic and cook for a further minute.
3 Preheat the oven to 180°C (350°F/Gas 4). Put the meat and onion in an ovenproof casserole dish, add the tomatoes, sugar, chilli, stock, vinegar, rosemary and drained beans. Cook, covered, for 2½ hours, until the meat is very tender.
4 Remove the rosemary sprig. Add the juice, zest and season to taste. Serve with thick crusty bread.

NUTRITION PER SERVE
Protein 55 g; Fat 20 g; Carbohydrate 20 g; Dietary Fibre 6 g; Cholesterol 165 mg; 1985 kJ (475 Cal)

The beans will soak up a lot of water so make sure they are well-covered.

Brown the meat in batches, draining it on paper towels.

The large sprig of fresh rosemary will give a distinctive flavour.

Find the sprig of rosemary and lift it out before serving the casserole.

COOK'S FILE

Variation: Use a 310 g (11 oz) can of butter beans (lima beans) instead. Add in the last 30 minutes of cooking.

CREAMY CHICKEN WITH MUSHROOMS

Preparation time: 20 minutes
Total cooking time: 40 minutes
Serves: 6

2 tablespoons olive oil
200 g (7 oz) button mushrooms, halved
200 g (7 oz) field mushrooms, chopped
1 small red capsicum (pepper), sliced
4 chicken breast fillets, cut into bite-sized pieces
2 tablespoons plain (all-purpose) flour
250 ml (1 cup) chicken stock
125 ml (1/2 cup) red wine
3 spring onions (scallions), finely chopped
300 ml (1 1/4 cups) cream
1/4 teaspoon turmeric
1 tablespoon chopped chives
1 tablespoon finely chopped fresh parsley

1 Heat the oil in a large pan and add the mushrooms and capsicum. Cook over medium heat for 4 minutes or until soft. Remove and set aside.

2 Brown the chicken quickly in batches over a medium-high heat. Sprinkle the pan with flour and cook for 2 minutes until golden. Add the stock and wine; bring to the boil. Cover and simmer for 10 minutes, or until the chicken is tender.

3 Add the spring onion and cream, return to the boil and simmer for 10–15 minutes, or until the cream has reduced and thickened. Return the mushrooms and capsicum to the pan; stir in the turmeric and herbs, season, then simmer for 5 minutes to heat.

NUTRITION PER SERVE
Protein 22 g; Fat 30 g; Carbohydrate 6 g; Dietary Fibre 2 g; Cholesterol 110 mg; 1670 kJ (400 Cal)

Choose large field mushrooms and wipe them with a damp cloth before chopping.

Add the spring onions and cream and return to the boil.

Add the mushrooms, capsicum, chives, parsley and turmeric.

COUNTRY BEEF STEW

Preparation time: 40 minutes
Total cooking time: 2 hours 10 minutes
Serves 8

1 small eggplant (aubergine), cubed
2–3 tablespoons olive oil
2 red onions, sliced
2 garlic cloves, crushed
1 kg (2 lb 4 oz) chuck steak, cubed
1 teaspoon ground coriander
1/2 teaspoon allspice
3/4 teaspoon sweet paprika
6 ripe tomatoes, chopped
250 ml (1 cup) red wine
750 ml (3 cups) beef stock
2 tablespoons tomato paste (purée)
250 g (9 oz) baby new potatoes, halved
2 sticks celery, sliced
3 carrots, chopped
2 bay leaves
15 g (1/4 cup) chopped parsley

1 Put the eggplant in a colander, sprinkle generously with salt and leave for 20 minutes. Rinse, pat dry with paper towels and set aside.

2 Heat the oil in a large pan and cook the onion for 5 minutes until soft; add the garlic and cook for 1 minute. Remove. Add the eggplant and brown for 5 minutes. Remove. Brown the meat in batches, sprinkle with spices, season and cook for 1–2 minutes. Add the tomato, onion, wine, stock and paste; bring to the boil. Reduce the heat and simmer, covered, for 25 minutes.

3 Add the potato, celery, carrot and bay leaves, bring to the boil, reduce the heat, cover and simmer for 1 hour. Add the eggplant and simmer for 30 minutes, uncovered. Remove the bay leaves and stir in the parsley.

NUTRITION PER SERVE
Protein 30 g; Fat 10 g; Carbohydrate 10 g; Dietary Fibre 4 g; Cholesterol 85 mg; 1160 kJ (280 Cal)

Put the eggplant in a colander and sprinkle with salt to draw out any bitterness.

Add the tomato, onion, wine, stock and tomato paste to the pan.

Add the potato, celery, carrot and bay leaves to the pan.

RICH STEAK AND KIDNEY STEW

Preparation time: 35 minutes
Total cooking time: 2 hours 30 minutes
Serves 4–6

1 kg (2 lb 4 oz) chuck steak
2–3 tablespoons oil
1 thick rasher bacon, rind removed and thinly sliced
40 g ($1\frac{1}{2}$ oz) butter
1 large onion, chopped
300 g ($10\frac{1}{2}$ oz) button mushrooms
250 ml (1 cup) brown muscat
2–3 garlic cloves, crushed
$\frac{1}{4}$ teaspoon ground allspice
$\frac{1}{2}$ teaspoon paprika
2 teaspoons coriander seeds, lightly crushed
8 lamb kidneys (425 g/15 oz), quartered, cores removed
1 tablespoon wholegrain mustard
250 ml (1 cup) beef or vegetable stock
2–3 tablespoons soft brown sugar
1–2 teaspoons fresh thyme
1–2 teaspoons fresh rosemary

1 Trim the steak of excess fat and sinew; cut into 2–3 cm ($\frac{3}{4}$–$1\frac{1}{2}$ inch) cubes. Heat 1 teaspoon of the oil in a large heavy-based pan. Add the bacon and cook for 2–3 minutes until just crisp; remove. Add 2 tablespoons oil and 30 g (1 oz) butter to the pan. Brown the steak in batches then remove from the pan and set aside.

2 Add the onion to the pan and cook for 2–3 minutes until soft and golden. Add the mushrooms and cook, stirring, for 3 minutes, until just brown. Stir in half the muscat and simmer for 3–4 minutes. Remove from the pan.

3 Add the remaining oil and butter to the pan. Stir in the garlic, allspice, paprika and coriander seeds and cook for 1 minute. Add the kidneys and cook, stirring, over medium heat until just beginning to brown. Stir in the remaining muscat and mustard and simmer for 2 minutes. Return the mushroom and onion mixture to the pan, with the steak and bacon. Stir until combined. Stir in the stock. Bring to the boil, reduce the heat, cover and simmer for 1 hour. Stir in the sugar (the amount depends on the sweetness of the muscat), cover and simmer for 40 minutes. Uncover and simmer for 20 minutes. Stir in the thyme and rosemary during the last 10 minutes.

NUTRITION PER SERVE (6)
Protein 50 g; Fat 20 g; Carbohydrate 12 g; Dietary Fibre 2 g; Cholesterol 365 mg; 1825 kJ (435 Cal)

Cut under and up to remove the attached inner cores from the kidneys.

When the mushrooms start to brown stir in half the muscat.

Return the browned steak and bacon to the pan and stir in the stock.

INDEX

USEFUL INFORMATION

All our recipes are thoroughly tested in a special test kitchen. Standard metric measuring cups and spoons are used in the development of our recipes. All cup and spoon measurements are level. We have used 60 g (2¼ oz/Grade 3) eggs in all recipes. Sizes of cans vary between manufacturers and countries—use the can size closest to the one suggested in the recipe.

Conversion Guide

1 cup	= 250 ml (9 fl oz)
1 teaspoon	= 5 ml
1 Australian tablespoon	= 20 ml (4 teaspoons)
1 UK/US tablespoon	= 15 ml (3 teaspoons)

Dry Measures		Liquid Measures		Linear Measures	
30 g	= 1 oz	30 ml	= 1 fl oz	6 mm	= ¼ inch
250 g	= 9 oz	125 ml	= 4 fl oz	1 cm	= ½ inch
500 g	= 1 lb 2 oz	250 ml	= 9 fl oz	2.5 cm	= 1 inch

Cup Conversions—Dry Ingredients

1 cup almonds, slivered = 125 g (4½ oz)

1 cup cheese, grated, lightly packed:

natural Cheddar = 125 g (4½ oz)

processed cheddar = 155 g (5½ oz)

Parmesan, Romano = 125 g (4½ oz)

1 cup flour = 125 g (4½ oz)

1 cup minced pork or beef = 250 g (9 oz)

1 cup pasta shapes = 125 g (4½ oz)

1 cup rice, shortgrain, raw = 200 g (7 oz)

1 cup sesame seeds = 160 g (6 oz)

1 cup split peas = 250 g (9 oz)

Oven Temperatures

In the following temperature ranges, the lower temperature applies to gas ovens, the higher to electric ovens. This is to allow for the fact that the flame in gas ovens generates a drier heat, which effectively cooks food faster than the moister heat of an electric oven, even if the temperature setting is the same.

	°C	°F	Gas Mark
Very slow	120	250	½
Slow	150	300	2
Mod slow	160	325	3
Moderate	180	350	4
Mod hot	190(g) – 210(e)	375 – 415	5
Hot	200(g) – 240(e)	400 – 475	6
Very hot	230(g) – 260(e)	450 – 525	8

(g) = gas (e) = electric

Note: For fan-forced ovens check your appliance manual, but as a general rule, set oven temperature to 20°C lower than the temperature indicated in the recipe.

International Glossary

chick pea	garbanzo bean
chilli	chili pepper, chile
cornflour	cornstarch
eggplant	aubergine
soft brown sugar	light brown sugar
spring onion	scallion
zucchini	courgette

This edition published in 2008 by Bay Books, an imprint of Murdoch Books Pty Limited.
Pier 8/9, 23 Hickson Road, Millers Point, NSW 2000, Australia

Editorial Director: Diana Hill. **Production Coordinator:** Liz Fitzgerald.
Managing Editor: Susan Tomnay. **Creative Director:** Marylouise Brammer.
Photo Librarian: Dianne Bedford. **Food Editors:** Kerry Ray, Tracy Rutherford.
Designer: Wing Ping Tong. **Recipe Development:** Jo Richardson, Sally Parker, Michelle Earl, Kerrie Ray, Jane Croswell-Jones, Maria Samponis, Tracy Rutherford.
Home Economists: Michelle Lawton, Wendy Goggin, Jo Forrest, Kerrie Mullins.
Photography: Jon Bader. **Step-by-step Photography:** Reg Morrison.
Food Stylist: Carolyn Fienberg. **Food Preparation:** Jo Forrest.
Chief Executive: Juliet Rogers. **Publisher:** Kay Scarlett.

ISBN 978 0 681 24548 8
Printed by Sing Cheong Printing Co. Ltd. PRINTED IN CHINA.

Copyright© Text, design, photography and illustrations Murdoch Books 1996. All rights reserved. No part of this publication may be reproduced, stored in a retrieval system or transmitted in any form or by any means, electronic, mechanical, photocopying, recording or otherwise without the prior written permission of the publisher.

1 cm 2 cm 3 cm 4 cm 5 cm 6 cm 7 cm 8 cm 9 cm 10 cm 11 cm 12 cm 13 cm 14 cm 15 cm 16 cm 17 cm 18 cm 19 cm 20 cm 21 cm 22 cm 23 cm 24 cm 25 cm